KENYA

a priority on my bucket list

DONNA KASIK

GlobalEdAdvance
Press

KENYA – A Priority on my Bucket List

Copyright © 2012 by Donna Kasik

Library of Congress Control Number:2012931574

Kasik, Donna 1961—

KENYA –A Priority on my Bucket List

ISBN 978-1-935434-63-4

Subject Codes and Description: 1. REL: 045000: Religion: Christian Ministry – Missions; 2. REL: 116000: Religion: Intolerance, Persecution & Conflict; 3. REL: 063000: Religion: Christian Life – Stewardship and Giving.

The writer acknowledges the editorial assistance of Joshua Collins and geaPress. All rights reserved, including the right to reproduce this book or any part thereof in any form, except for inclusion of brief quotations in a review, without the written permission of the author and GlobalEdAdvancePRESS.

Printed in Australia, Brazil, France, Germany, Italy, Spain, UK, and USA.

Book Cover Design by Barton Green

The Press does not have ownership of the contents of a book; this is the author's work and the author owns the copyright. All theories, concepts, constructs, and perspectives are those of the author and not necessarily the Press. They are presented for open and free discussion of the issues involved. All comments and feedback should be directed to the Email: [comments4author@aol.com] and the comments will be forwarded to the author for response.

Published by

GlobalEdAdvance Press

DEDICATION

This book is dedicated to all of my dear friends and students in Kenya who, through their great love for God and for others, and by their deep faith, gave me a new love and appreciation for Africa.

Also, specifically, to Kibii and Esther, Nebert and Jane, and my dear friends Josephine and Nathan Chesang.

Most importantly, thank you Nathan; through your unwavering faith in our Savior, you showed me what a true Christ-follower looks like. Thank you for your loyal friendship, and for your help with this book; it could not have been written without you.

Table of Contents

~

Prologue	**Prioritizing my Bucket List**	9
Chapter 1	**Thinking Globally**	11
Chapter 2	**Beginning the Journey**	17
Chapter 3	**Returning to Kenya**	43
Chapter 4	**Learning through Change**	63
Chapter 5	**Confronting Cultural Differences**	85
Chapter 6	**Challenging the Church**	111
Chapter 7	**Developing a Mission Policy**	127
Chapter 8	**Dreaming Big**	139
References		143

"And let us not become weary in doing what is right; for if we do not weaken our resolve, in due season we will collect the good harvest. As we have opportunity, let us practice generosity to all, especially those who are of the household of faith."

(Galatians 6:9-10 DNT)

PROLOGUE

Prioritizing my Bucket List

Many of us have a bucket list, a list of things we want to do or accomplish before we die. One of the items on my bucket list was to go somewhere in Africa, which included a safari. I wanted to ride around in the open plains and see the wild animals out in their natural habitat. I can now scratch Africa off of my bucket list, including the safari; but, little did I know that Africa (specifically Kenya), would become a second home to me and would offer far more than a safari ride. In prioritizing my bucket list, Kenya was moved to the top of my list.

I have friends who live in the Chicago area named Jim and Henny, who used to be missionaries for many years in Kenya, along with their four children. When I first met them, I expressed a love for Africa and a desire to go there. We quickly became friends, and the next thing I knew they began planning a trip for me to Kenya.

After Sunday school one day, Jim and I walked down the hallway of the church, and he asked me, "How would you like to go to Kenya on a mission trip?" I replied, "Oh, you know I would love to go!" "Well then, you'll go!" Not really believing him, I responded with a glib, "O.K." That was the end of the conversation-or so I thought. My adventure began and became an experience of which there is no comparison. Within that year I found myself alone in Africa, and I loved it.

Are missions on your bucket list?

Kenya

"All authority has been committed to Me in heaven and in earth. As you personally go, (going) therefore, make disciples of all nations, baptizing them in the name of the Father, and of the Son, and of the Holy Spirit, teaching them to observe all things whatever I have commanded you: and behold, I am with you always, even unto the end of the world. Amen."

(Matthew 28:19-20 DNT).

1

THINKING GLOBALLY

Kenya

I, an American, have traveled to Kenya seven times, and I became close friends with some people who helped me begin to understand the Kenyan way of thinking, and how the Kenyan Church operates. My friend Nathan graciously invited me to his home many times to talk about a clash of cultures between Americans and Kenyans, and to show me a ministry that he directs, but which was beginning to fall apart because of cultural misunderstandings in partnership with Americans.

As I hoped to learn from others' mistakes, and unfortunately through some of my own mistakes, I took back to America what I learned in Kenya, to help Nathan rebuild a wonderful ministry through the love and assistance of the American Church. I also realized how difficult it can be to live cross-culturally, and how many hurtful mistakes can be made, all in the name of Christ and with our best intentions. Come, and through these pages, travel with me to Kenya as we hopefully learn together for the glory of Christ and the increase of His Kingdom.

The Great Commission

What does it mean to think globally, and why should we do so? To think globally means to think outside of the immediate world around us: our town, our county, our state, and even our country. As Christians, we are commanded to think globally. In

Jesus' last words on earth, known as *The Great Commission*, we read,

> *"And Jesus came and spoke, saying, 'All authority has been committed to Me in heaven and in earth. As you personally go, (going) therefore, make disciples of all nations, baptizing them in the name of the Father, and of the Son, and of the Holy Spirit, teaching them to observe all things whatever I have commanded you: and behold, I am with you always, even unto the end of the world. Amen'"* (Matthew 28:19-20 DNT).

Of all the final instructions Jesus could have given, why did He choose these words as His final teaching to us? Jesus must have thought that the idea of missions and global outreach was important. While of course it is important to evangelize, to help, and to live as missionaries in our own communities, Jesus commanded us to reach out into other areas as well.

The Apostle Paul

In Paul's missionary journeys, he traveled most of the known world at that time, preaching the Gospel of Jesus Christ, and he started churches and fellowships wherever he went. Paul also did an important thing that we as a Church do not often practice; he collected money from wealthier churches to give to poorer churches in other countries. In the book of Romans, chapter 15, Paul wrote to those in Italy:

> *"Previously I have been hindered from coming to you. But now since the work here is completed, and having a great desire for many years to come to you; when I travel to Spain, I will visit you: for I hope to include you in my journey and be aided forward after I have enjoyed your company for a while. But first I must go to Jerusalem to deliver a collection to the saints. For the provinces of Macedonia and Achaia have freely made a contribution for the poor saints in Jerusalem. It was a pleasure for the Gentiles, being debtors and partakers of spiritual things, to feel responsible to minister in material things. When I have finished this task and assured the delivery of the collection, I plan to visit you on my way to Spain. And I*

am certain that when I visit you it will be in the fullness of the blessing of the gospel of Christ" (Romans 15:22-29 DNT).

Paul stated as a matter of fact, without dispute, that churches in particular parts of the world which have been blessed materially and financially (such as the churches in Greece which he mentioned), are indebted to give to other churches in poorer countries, such as the church Paul mentioned in Israel, which was rich in faith and able to bless others through their faith, but which lacked resources. If the Church is one Body in Christ, then are we not to assist one another? Paul traveled from country to country as he visited wealthy churches who gave him money to help poor churches in other countries. According to Scripture, what then is the obligation of the American Church? As a rich country with one of the highest standards of living in the world, should we as Christians not follow the example of Paul?

American Arguments

Some Americans may argue that there are also many poor people in this country, and that we need to care for them, perhaps first. While this economic fact remains true, the poorest American is envied by many of the poorest of the poor in Third World countries. America has some wealthy churches, and even many churches of modest income have food pantries, clothes closets, extra money to share, dinners to host, and some churches even offer shelter for the homeless.

Americans have government programs such as food stamps, public housing, medical cards, welfare checks, unemployment compensation, social security, disability, etc. Third World countries do not have these types of government programs. People literally starve to death. People die from treatable diseases since they have no access to medical care or clean water. Homeless, orphaned children roam the streets, begging, while others, if "fortunate," find food in the garbage dumps. While it is indeed true that some Americans go hungry, no one needs to starve to death in this country; there is help, somewhere, that can be found.

Can Americans continue to turn a blind eye to those suffering in other countries, including fellow brothers and sisters in the Lord? Jesus said in Matthew 25 that if we do not feed the hungry, clothe the naked, visit those sick and in prison, welcome the stranger, and give water to the thirsty, then we are also not doing that for Him (Matthew 25:31-46). When Jesus made this statement concerning helping and serving others, He did not place boarders on where we are to help. Jesus did not place boarders on compassion. In the entirety of Scripture, including the Great Commission, and following the example of Paul, we as a Church are to think, act, and live globally; it is that simple. If we do not want to reach out to those outside of our community, then we do not want to follow Jesus.

Missions

In his address at the 2010 Lausanne Conference (a global church missions conference), John Piper made a strong and accurate statement concerning missions. Piper said that we have three options: go, send, or disobey. According to Jesus' last words as He was leaving this earth, Piper is correct. Jesus said,

"As you personally go, (going) therefore, and make disciples of all nations, baptizing them in the name of the Father, and of the Son, and of the Holy Spirit: teaching them to observe all things whatever I have commanded you" (Matthew 28:19-20a DNT).

Jesus spoke those words, recorded in Matthew, to His followers, that as they were going, His command was for them to make disciples, and it was not spoken as a suggestion or as an option. It was an imperative!

So where do we begin in this venture of love and obedience through missions? Too often many of us have tried, and our best intentions have failed and hurt others because we did not know how to serve, we were not culturally sensitive, and we did not bother to learn how another culture thinks, behaves, lives, etc. This book is about one country, Kenya, and some of the cultural considerations that are necessary in trying to serve there, which are also applicable to serving in other parts of the world.

We all make mistakes when we are unaware and insensitive to other ways of life. All people have many similarities since we share in a common humanity, but we have different ways of living out our humanity, and we can unknowingly cause pain and misunderstandings even amongst Christians with the best of intentions.

Many American missionaries also have the idea that mission work involves reaching *down* to others to help bring them *up,* unaware that this attitude is elitist and arrogant, and hurts people. Missionaries from any race and culture, who go to another race and culture unlike their own, are there to serve and to learn from others, as well as to give of themselves and to do whatever work it is they came to do.

Mission work is always a two-way street of love, service, learning, teaching and assistance, while intentionally learning another culture, accepting that culture as one's own, and always being culturally sensitive, which is a long and arduous process. Mission work involves building loving, respectful and trusting relationships with people from another culture, teaching others about Jesus, and allowing the indigenous people to learn and discover their own talents and gifts, in order to serve their own people.

Let the Church and her people "think globally!" Amen!

KENYA

"We often fear that which we do not know
or understand."

2

BEGINNING THE JOURNEY

The Adventure Begins

The travel to Africa was long and exhausting: eight hours from Chicago to London with a planned twelve-hour lay-over to tour the city, and then another eight hours from London to Nairobi, Kenya. My travels began with two other people from the church who I did not really know (a husband and wife named Dana and Karmen), and we enjoyed getting acquainted during our travels. While both Dana and Karmen had traveled extensively, neither had been to Africa before, so we were all excited. This couple would be staying in a different part of Kenya than I was, but at least we were together for the traveling. We would later meet Jim in London for the second half of the journey to Nairobi.

The three of us arrived in London and boarded the "tube," which is the subway in London. We saw Big Ben, the London Bridge, Piccadilly Circus, the London Eye, Buckingham Palace, Westminster Abbey, Winston Churchill's War Room, and many other interesting sights of the city. After walking all over London, we went to a nice Italian restaurant for lunch and feasted on some warm bread, spaghetti, spinach, wine, and chocolates. We all enjoyed ourselves. Life was good and plentiful.

After lunch, we walked back to the "tube" to head back to the airport. By this time, I felt tired, dirty, and in need of a shower. What a nice surprise to discover that for about five American dollars I could take a hot, private shower at the airport! Clean, refreshed, and ready for Africa, we soon met Jim at the London airport who had just come in from the Middle East from some mission work. The four of us boarded the huge 747 airplane that held 450 people, which was filled to capacity, and we were packed in like sardines. I was exhausted and settled into my seat for the rest of the journey.

Kenya

We finally arrived in Nairobi, Kenya, East Africa. Jim had arranged for a van to pick us up, and we were driven to a Wycliffe guest house that Bible translators, like Jim, stayed at while in Kenya. The guest house was simple, but adequate. I shared a room with a woman named Tammy who flew in from Portland, Oregon, but had not yet arrived in Nairobi; she would join us later that night. There were two bathrooms in this area of the guest house that about ten people shared, but we had a nice shower, the rooms were clean with small twin beds, and the grounds were beautiful.

After cleaning up, Jim and I took a walk to visit some of his missionary friends, while Dana and Karmen took a nap. I was anxious to see as much of Nairobi as possible, so I welcomed the walk. We had a lovely visit with the missionary family that Jim knew, as we drank some refreshing homemade lemonade and shared stories. I had become exhausted from the travel and jet lag, and I began to wish I had stayed back for a nap.

We finally left Jim's friends, and as we walked back to the guest house, another one of Jim's friends, a Kenyan woman, drove past and called out excitedly to Jim since it had been several years since she had seen him. Jim told her we were staying at the Wycliffe guest house, and she said she would take us back to the guest house to pick up Dana and Karmen and bring all of us back to her home for dinner. I wanted to excuse myself from this invitation, but I knew I could not, so I prayed for strength. Dana and Karmen got up feeling refreshed, and we drove about twenty minutes to this woman's home.

Not having been to Kenya before, I quickly noticed that all of the houses, schools, hotels, etc. are gated, locked, and have walls that surround these areas. Every building is within a gated compound, and a gate-keeper lets visitors in and out at his discretion. I also noticed that all of the windows had bars on the outside. I began to think of my safety....

When we arrived at this Kenyan woman's home, she was kind and hospitable, and made us feel most welcomed. She worked as a nurse, and her husband was out of town at this time on business. The house was small, but clean and comfortable, and filled with people. She often had people at her home to eat and sleep, sometimes as many as fourteen at one time! All five of her children were hard workers with good educations, and she was very proud of her family.

For lunch, we ate beans, rice, greens, bananas and oranges, which were quite good. I was so tired though, that I began to feel sick. All I could think of was sleep, which I had not had for a long time now. Two hours later we drank chai, which is a delicious tea mixed with milk and sugar, which in Kenya, is drunk several times a day, including after meals. Finally, Jim said it was time to go home, and we got a ride back to the guest house where we all enjoyed a great nap for about three hours.

I was still a student in seminary at the time of this trip, so I stayed at the guest house to do some homework while Jim, Dana and Karmen walked to a small street market to get us some dinner. They came back with papayas, bananas, mangos, and carrots which we had to wash in boiled bleach water prior to eating to kill any bacteria to prevent us from getting sick. We all stood around the kitchen and prepared the fresh produce while we watched the cockroaches scatter about. Shortly after we ate, we each went to bed for a much needed sleep. I awoke several times to strange noises throughout the night which sounded like elephants to me; who knows what they were–I did not care; I was in Kenya!

In the morning I took a nice shower and then went to the dining area for breakfast. We were served mango, bread, jam, coffee and tea. After breakfast, our driver arrived to take us on our seven hour drive to Kitale. I was happy to take this long drive since it was a wonderful opportunity to see a large portion of the country. Much of Kenya is beautiful, with lush, green areas, including the Great Rift Valley, and I thoroughly enjoyed the drive. We stopped at an outdoor café that was connected to a gas station for lunch, where, as a vegetarian, I could not find much to eat, but, I enjoyed a piece of banana bread and some mango. Since I had some money in my pocket, I always seemed to find something to eat and never went hungry.

A Different World

The roads in Kenya are terrible, and the driving is crazy. The dirt paths that are called "roads" are narrow and bumpy, filled with huge craters which the Kenyans call "potholes." In fear, I watched as cars sped by to pass along winding, narrow mountain roads while oncoming traffic appeared to be heading straight towards us. We drove past a semi-truck flipped over in a ditch, lying upside down, probably as a result of this maniacal driving. The drive was scary, but we appeared to have a relatively good, safe driver. I did, however, wear my seat belt and I prayed as we rode along the Kenyan countryside.

Poverty everywhere; I have been in the inner cities of America and I have even lived in them. I thought I saw poverty before, but not this level of poverty. I looked at mud huts with grass roofs, and small, wood and metal shacks. There was no electricity. There was no plumbing. There was no heat or air-conditioning. There were not even any windows in some of the homes. There were no kitchens, no bathrooms–nothing. My heart ached at the level of this extreme poverty. I thought back to the guest house with the little twin beds and the shared bathroom with gratefulness. I thought about my house back home in the Chicago suburbs, almost with shame. I was in Africa.

We finally arrived in Kitale and went to the home of Brian and Heather, a missionary family from Texas. They worked at the seminary where I would be teaching for the next ten days. This missionary family had a nice, large, clean house (gated of course), in a beautiful compound. We were all introduced to them and their children, we visited for a while, and then my four other traveling companions, Jim, Tammy, Dana and Karmen left me to go to their work area on Mt. Elgon. I suddenly felt alone.

I talked with this young family for a while, but in the back of my mind I wondered where I would be staying for the next couple of weeks. Would I stay at their house? Would I stay in a mud and grass hut, or in a wood or metal shack? I had no idea where I would stay, since my living arrangements were not discussed before I arrived. After about a half hour, Brian said, "Well, I guess I'll take you to the seminary where you will be staying." I wondered what it would be like. We drove for about ten minutes on dirt roads filled with craters (I mean potholes), and reached the compound where the seminary was located. The gate-keeper recognized Brian and let us in with a warm smile. Brian showed me around the compound and then took me to my cottage. The view from the seminary compound was beautiful; it overlooked the mountains, and there were flowers, grass, and trees everywhere. I felt good.

My New Home

The cottage was a large house with several bedrooms and bathrooms (which included running water, showers, and toilets, though toilet paper was often scarce). It had a communal kitchen and living room, and an enclosed front porch where a clothes-line hung so I could hang my laundry, which I would wash by hand in the yard. The kitchen had a small propane stove that looked like a Coleman camp stove, a small refrigerator stocked with sodas and bottled water, eggs, cereal, peanut butter and boxed milk. There was a sink with running water, a coffee pot with coffee and filters, and, of course, tea and sugar.

I was pleasantly surprised at my new home for the next couple of weeks. Brian welcomed me to the cottage, told me to unpack and relax, and said that he would come by and get me in the morning to take me to my classroom and introduce me to my students. Brian reminded me to make sure I was locked in at night, which meant locking the padlock of the gated door in front of the large wooden door of the cottage. Perhaps I looked a little nervous, I am not sure, since Brian then said, "Oh, don't worry. The compound is locked at night and there is always a gate keeper in front. Dogs are also let out to roam the compound at night, along with a guard armed with a bow and arrows. You'll be safe." With a smile, Brian gave me the keys and wished me a peaceful night.

My First Night in Kenya

I had the entire cottage to myself, and I enjoyed the privacy; however, it also felt a bit lonely. I picked out a bedroom and began to unpack. I looked through my lesson plans for the following morning and I began to get nervous. I was not a teacher, and I had never even taught before. I worked as a painter in the construction trades, and I attended seminary classes at night. Would my students be able to tell that I was not a teacher? Would I appear nervous? What was I doing here all alone in Africa? Why did I agree to come and teach? I began to have second thoughts. I just wanted to see the animals out on safari-not teach a group of pastors at a seminary! Suddenly, I wanted to be back home. I was tired and nervous, so at about 9:00 p.m. I decided to go to bed. I secured the mosquito net over me as I had been instructed at the guest house to help prevent malaria (which is rampant in many parts of Africa), and quickly fell asleep.

At 10:45 p.m. I was awakened by the sound of at least two men talking right outside of my bedroom window, and dogs running up and down my porch, barking. I could not understand what the men were saying to one another since they were speaking in Swahili, but I could pick out a word here and there which I had learned, and I knew they said that there was a white woman staying in this cottage alone. My mind raced and fear swept over me like a hurricane. I lay motionless in my bed, prayed, and dared not even move, as I hoped the men would not know which bedroom was mine. Here I was in Africa, a dream come true, and I felt like I would not live past my first night alone! What happened to that promise of safety and security from Brian? The men walked all around my cottage several times, then up the steps of the porch to the door, and stood. As I laid and listened to these men and the dogs, waiting for them to break in at any second, in my prayers, fears, and exhaustion, I finally fell back asleep.

Incorrect Assumptions

The morning finally came, and with the first sign of sunlight, my alarm went off. I was thankful to still be alive. I went to the kitchen but forgot to put on my glasses. I have poor eyesight, and in the darkened room and blurriness of my vision, I saw a rather large black creature run past me on the counter. I had always envisioned large black spiders in Africa, like tarantulas or something, and supposing this is what was in my kitchen, I took my fist and smashed it. I heard and felt a crunch. Yuck! Whatever it was though, it was dead. I went and got my glasses, turned on some lights, and to my surprise, there laid a squashed lizard. I was later told that lizards are a good thing to have in one's home in Kenya since they eat mosquitoes, which carry malaria. It occurred to me that I was probably still a bit on edge from the previous night's scare. We often fear that which we do not know or understand. I was also thankful for the lights in my cottage.

I continued my morning routine and made coffee, exercised, read my Bible, and had a quick run through the compound. I ate breakfast and took a shower in what Brian called a "Mr. Coffee for humans" since the water pressure was so low, but it felt good none the less. Once again, I went over my lesson plan for the day and prayed, a lot, since I was nervous. A few minutes before 8:00 a.m. Brian came to the cottage as he promised, to take me to my classroom. He asked how my night was, and I relayed the story of the men and the dogs. Brian began to laugh, which I thought was rather rude. He then apologized for not informing me that he had asked two guards to keep a special watch on my cottage since I was a single, American lady staying alone in this cottage. How relieved and foolish I felt, but also a bit upset that I went through all of that fear unnecessarily. Brian apologized, and we both had a good laugh out of the story.

The African Seminary

Brian and I walked over to the classrooms, and there sat about fifteen Kenyan pastors, eagerly awaiting my presence. I was introduced, and then left alone in this room of men waiting to learn something from me to help them in their ministries. To my relief, I was only nervous for a few minutes since these men had such warm smiles and made me feel so welcomed. I began to relax and started the class, which went well. I taught for an hour-and-a-half until it was time to go to chapel. My students asked me to join them in chapel, and I gladly accepted. There were about three or four other classes going on in addition to mine, who all came together for chapel; then the singing began. Most of the students were men, but there were also a few women. The singing was unbelievably beautiful and passionate. These students/pastors obviously loved to worship. I was caught up in the sounds of praise to our God. I felt God's presence so strongly in this beautiful music, and I thought about how we were all part of the same family- the family of believers in Jesus Christ.

After the singing, one of my students came up front to preach. On my first impression, this particular student appeared unfriendly, but as I listened to him preach I began to feel drawn to him. My first impression was quite wrong. How often do I judge something or someone incorrectly? Probably more times than I care to admit. After the sermon, another one of my students asked me to share. I went up front and read from Colossians 1 and spoke about the fact that we are all brothers and sisters in Christ, with one Father, and we can all learn from one another. I told these students how anxious I was to learn from them, and hopefully they would learn something from me as well. Surprisingly, I was not at all nervous, but felt comfortable speaking in the midst of my new Kenyan friends.

When chapel concluded, it was time for *chai* (tea), and we all walked down to the dining hall. The tea was delicious. We laughed and talked with one another, and enjoyed our new relationship. After the tea break, we went back to class for another two hours of teaching. I felt confident and was enjoying myself. God heard and answered my prayers, and I quickly learned that when we do not have what we feel we need, God provides for us in amazing ways. Though I prepared long and hard to teach this class, I was nervous and I lacked confidence. God supplied all of my needs, in great abundance, and I was even having fun! God provided above and beyond what I expected. I then remembered a saying I once heard: "God does not send the equipped, but He equips those He sends."

When lunch-time came, my students and I walked down to the dining hall together. We stood in line, got our plates, and were served by the staff cooks from a long table in the front of the dining room. My students asked me to sit with them and talk, which I gladly did. Behind the dining hall were several outdoor sinks where we washed our dishes in cold water after we ate. I almost never washed my own dishes since my students delighted in taking turns washing them for me. On rare occasions, I would wash my own plate, and sometimes some of my student's plates (to return the favor). Lunch was usually beans, rice, and a banana, or lentil soup with chapatti, which was delicious, large, fried, flat bread. After lunch, I went back to my cottage to freshen up and I prepared for the two-hour homework assignment I was required to give each day. I also needed to be available for any questions, for help, and to begin grading my student's assignments.

Later that evening when I spoke with several of the seminary staff and some visiting teachers, I learned that most of my students did not have much education, and were from "the bush," or rural areas. In Kenya, one becomes a pastor, and *then* pursues his education, which is a much different system than America. I assumed that, since these men were in seminary, they had good educations, and I prepared to teach at the college level. I had since discovered that the students were at more of a Jr. High level. With this new knowledge of my students' education, I knew that I would need to make some adjustments to my course, and I prayed they would not be discouraged with my class. Teaching was great fun so far, but also rather challenging (especially in light of this new information), but by the grace of God, I prayed we would all learn and enjoy both the class and each other.

In the course of my teaching, I realized that I made an incorrect assumption. Since my students did not have the formal education that I had earlier assumed, I thought that they would not be able to comprehend some of the material I had planned on teaching. I was wrong. Just because they lacked the formal training, these pastors were extremely bright and they worked harder than most American students that I knew. My students readily understood the material, and most did quite well. Perhaps that elitist American mind-set crept in without my awareness; how easy that could happen! I felt ashamed....

Poverty – Up Close and Personal

Brian's wife Heather came to my cottage and picked me up after the study/homework period to take me to town. People everywhere were begging, and the poverty was gut-wrenching. I felt guilty going into the shops to buy something for myself, so I bought just a few pieces of fruit, bleach to wash the fruit in, juice, and some toilet paper. I asked Heather how she could tolerate living around such need, and she admitted that it was sometimes difficult.

Heather took me back to my cottage, and there I sat, alone, as I thought and wrote. However, I was no longer afraid as I was on that first night. Again, I had an arrogant, ignorant assumption that I should fear Kenyans, or fear being in Africa for some reason. I feared what I did not know. I was having a wonderful time and found my first overseas mission trip remarkable. I loved these people and this area of Kenya, with all of its natural beauty and the warmth and kindness of the people. I sat in the enclosed porch to grade papers, enjoyed the scenery, and quietly watched the African sun set behind the mountains.

I slept much better that night, without fear, and I woke up to my daily morning routine. As I took my morning jog, I thought of the incredibly strong faith of my students, which put my faith to shame. Most of my students literally had nothing, so they naturally depended on God for everything. Many Christians in America have far more than they need to live, and usually depend on personal resources and strength. Americans are also much more independent and over all, do not live in such a close community as the Kenyans. Kenyan families stay together. The oldest son is responsible to care for his mother, and she usually lives in his home when her husband dies, rather than alone or in a nursing home. My students were devoted to their families, to one another, and mostly, to God. They were eager to learn and to share whatever knowledge they acquired to teach others and to spread the good news of the Gospel of Jesus Christ. Since most of the students were already pastors, they also had a deep love and concern for their churches as well. I was humbled.

One of my students, Jackson, was from a primitive tribe called the Pokot. The people of this tribe are nomadic, and survive primarily on cow's milk and blood. They raid others' homes and land in order to steal their cattle. They live in homes of sticks, mud, and cow dung, and then often move every few days. After his education was completed, Jackson planned to go back to his tribal area so his people could hear about Jesus. Jackson would be placing his life at risk, since he would also need to explain that raiding, stealing, and killing are wrong, which would change this tribe's entire way of life.

Most of the students at this seminary placed their lives at risk when they spread their faith in Jesus, but they did so with joy because of their unwavering faith and love for God and others. Many of these students became Christians through the lives of missionaries, many American, which gave me a greater respect, appreciation, and awareness of the need for missionaries. I wondered how a missionary would be able to be culturally relevant and respectful to a tribe such as Jackson's, whose entire life-style would need to change if it became Christian; this cultural difficulty enabled me to understand the need to train people to be missionaries within their own country, and I was thankful to be a part of this process as their teacher, and to help equip pastors to work among their own tribes and people. An American has much to learn to be an effective missionary in the Pokot area.

When I told my students that I came from America just to teach this class and that I would be going home when it was completed, they were unanimously humbled and said they could not believe they were so important that someone would travel so far just for them. Though I kept this thought to myself, I felt a bit ashamed since part of the reason for coming to Kenya was simply to see Africa, fulfill a bucket list wish that I had, and to go on a safari; teaching this class was almost secondary at that particular point in my experience; fortunately, I began to develop a new perspective.

The students and I ate dinner together in the dining hall while I listened to them tell heart-breaking stories about all of the orphaned children on the streets of Kenya whose parents died from HIV AIDS. These AIDS orphans were left to fend for themselves, eating from trash and begging in the streets, as I had witnessed when I went to town with Heather. I saw skinny, dirty children who slept in the streets, wore rags, and had nowhere to go, nothing to do, and no one to love them. There were parts of this African adventure that were quite disturbing.

Going back to my cottage to grade papers and to do some of my own seminary homework, I heard the loud call to prayer from the Muslim mosque just down the street. I would have much rather heard the sound of the pastors singing in chapel.

The following day, I spoke to Susan, who was the cleaning lady at the seminary. She was a single mother of two children, and she walked over an hour each way to come to work here. Susan used to live with her mother and depended on her, but her mother recently died. I had no idea what happened to the father of Susan's children, and I did not ask. Susan expressed gratefulness for this job which enabled her to support herself and the children that "God blessed her with."

Susan said she needed to go clean my cottage, and I told her to help herself to whatever she wanted to eat in my kitchen. Susan told me that, when she was cleaning the other day, she saw some things that "looked good and sweet" in my kitchen and she was curious as to what they were. I asked her to show me what she saw, and she came out with some chocolate protein bars that I brought from home. I needed to get back to my class, so I told her to try one and to tell me what she thought. As I walked to my classroom, I was amazed that Susan never stole one protein bar. Susan was poor, and she had two children at home who I know she struggled to feed, but Susan was a Christian woman and lived according to the Word of God. After class I saw Susan and asked her how she liked the sweet treat, and she responded excitedly in the affirmative. I told her to come to the cottage, and I gave her the whole box to take home for her and her children. Susan was delighted; it was such a simple, inexpensive thing to do, but it meant so much to this woman. I was amazed.

Alone With God

Later that night as I sat alone in my cottage, I realized my brain was becoming tired and my emotions were all over the map. Never having taught a formal class before, teaching eight hours per day, then sitting in the classroom for two hours of study, questions, and homework, grading papers, and trying to keep up with my own seminary work was beginning to wear me down. I also felt quite alone. There was no radio, no television, and no company. Kenyan evenings consisted of me, my thoughts, my feelings, and my God. I wanted something to do besides read, write, and grade papers, but there *was* nothing else to do, and I barely had enough time to complete the work that I was required to do.

The next day, I met a visiting teacher named Nebert, who was staying in the cottage next door to me. He was Kenyan, and we discovered that we had a mutual friend from West Africa, who currently lived in America. What a small world! While I spoke to this Kenyan teacher (who was currently a Doctoral student at a seminary in America), he said he was amazed that my students told me what tribes they were from, especially Jackson from the Pokot tribe. Nebert told me that these students must have trusted me to give me this information, since normally students would not open up like that. I felt honored. Nebert and I also became friends, and remain good friends to this day.

I thought about the National Geographic television shows or magazine articles that spoke about these "primitive" people over in Africa, and how different they appeared from the world I knew; but here I was, face to face with these very people, who were really no different from me at all. While there will always be cultural differences between people, I realized that we are all so much more alike than we are different. We all have the same human needs, wants, desires, emotions, etc. We are all created in God's image. We all need Jesus. My loneliness began to fade.

Welcomed Diversions

The next day at tea time, my students and I were standing outside the dining hall drinking our chai, when I saw monkeys climbing around in the trees. I was excited and said I wanted to get my camera. My students lovingly laughed at me since sighting monkeys was a daily occurrence to them, though it was not for this Chicago area "teacher!" We had fun discovering each other's similarities and differences, but we delighted in the fact that we all loved and served Jesus.

The following day, Saturday, was a lovely day. Class ended at noon so some of the students could return home to their families and to their churches for Sunday worship. Brian's wife Heather came and picked me up again to take me shopping and I bought some beautiful souvenirs for my family and friends. Heather took me to some small, local shops where I purchased many items of soap stone, which is a beautiful, hard, shiny painted pottery made in Kenya. Heather's knowledge of the language, the currency, and the people also kept me from being ripped-off by the locals when they saw a "rich American." I loved my time so far in Kenya, but I wondered if I could live in such a poverty-stricken country for years like Heather and Brian, and like my friends Jim and Henny. I held a greater respect and admiration for these missionary friends.

Later that night, I awaited another missionary family to pick me up and take me to their home for dinner. Bill was a Caucasian man from Alabama who married a Kenyan woman he met while working as a missionary at an orphanage years ago in Kenya. I was grateful to have somewhere to go and people to talk to for an evening since it became increasingly more difficult to stay alone each evening in my cottage. Bill and his wife had three children, and it was fun to visit with a lively family. Bill was the Director of the seminary where I was teaching and he was able to share a lot of information and history concerning the seminary.

I was hungry and desired a change to my diet which consisted of the same thing every evening: *ugali* (a staple Kenyan food made from maize (corn) flour and water), greens and cabbage. I also longed for something sweet like chocolate, since I gave Susan all of my chocolate protein bars. Bill's wife cooked pork chops (which I apologized for not eating since I am a vegetarian), potato salad, green beans, carrots, home-made dinner rolls, and for desert, ice cream and brownies!

What a wonderful meal. I thanked them both over and over for the delicious meal and the company, which I truly appreciated. After dinner, their children retrieved toy instruments, passed them out to each of us, and we all sang Bible songs together while we played our instruments. I had such fun. After the children went to bed, Bill and his wife showed me around their beautiful compound and we spoke of the seminary, the students, and our faith. I listened attentively to Bill's stories of living in Africa, which he loved. I had a wonderful day.

Mt. Elgon

The next day, Sunday, I was scheduled to go to Mt. Elgon with Brian to see my American friends with whom I traveled. I was so excited since I was beginning to feel pretty homesick, and spending the day with my American friends would be just what I needed. I would also have the chance to join them for church. As I poured the milk on my breakfast cereal, the gatekeeper knocked at my door to tell me that Brian was on the phone for me. I went up to the front office to get the phone, and Brian said that his wife was ill and was up most of the night vomiting, so he could not take me to Mt. Elgon. I felt terrible that Heather was so sick, but I also selfishly felt terrible that I could not go to the mountain and see my friends. Here I was, thinking about myself again. This day was certainly going to be long since most of the students had left for the weekend and everyone who knew me here was aware that I already had plans to go to Mt. Elgon; therefore, I would not be receiving any invitations to go anywhere.

The offices of the seminary were closed, I had no phone numbers, and I would be left to sit alone in the compound all day, disappointed, with nothing to do. All of the grading was done, and my own homework was completed. I felt myself fighting my self-centeredness, and I attempted to stop thinking about my day and think about Heather who was sick (but I was having a difficult time doing so). Brian apologized, and I told him I understood, but I think he detected my frustration, or he probably understood my situation, as an American himself. He asked if I would feel safe taking a taxi. "Sure," I said, "Unless I have reason not to?" Brian told me he would call a taxi driver he knew well and trusted, though the trip would take about 1.5 hours and would be expensive. At this point, I did not care–I just wanted to go, so I asked him to call the taxi driver and I would be ready. Brian said he would call me back in a half hour to confirm.

I went back to my cottage and excitedly finished my breakfast, then returned to the office to wait for his call. Brian secured a driver for me, and Bill's wife (the family whose home I ate dinner at the previous night) would be coming with me since she was somewhat familiar with the area, and the driver was not. I was so thankful that God provided a way for me to see my friends and to leave the compound for the day.

I had envisioned my friends up on a remote mountain without much food or anything, so I decided to bring them the home-made cinnamon rolls "Mrs. Bill" (what the Kenyan's called Bill's wife) gave me to take home and share. I also stopped and bought some chocolate toffee and dried apricots so they would have a treat. I was sure my missionary friends were hungry and in need of some goodies.

The drive lasted about 1.5 hours, with the last half hour on steep dirt roads as our car ascended the mountain. None of us were sure where my friends were specifically located, so the driver stopped and asked everyone who was walking where the muzungu's (white people) were, and where the Bible translating center was. No one could tell us about the center, but many people were able to direct us to the muzungu's. The mountain was beautiful, but again, extreme poverty was all around.

Finally, we arrived at the Bible translation center, and Tammy, my former roommate, waited outside the church for me. My other three friends were in the church, which was about a five minute walk from where she was waiting. I told Tammy that I brought them some treats, so she brought me to the house where she was staying to drop them off and thanked me.

I could not believe what I saw. My friends were living in a nice, two-story house with a large kitchen, stocked with all kinds of food and treats. This house is where Jim and Henny lived with their four children when they were full-time missionaries here in Kenya. Tammy was the only one of my four friends though, who was allowed to sleep in the house since two, single, American missionary women lived there and no men were allowed. Dana and Karmen slept in a small bunker house next door that had no plumbing or electricity, but had plenty of spiders, and Jim slept in a similar apartment type of building about a block away. They were all allowed however, to eat their meals in the house and use the bathroom and shower.

After a tour of the house, we walked to the church. I could not believe the way these people lived; their standard of living was unlike any poverty in America. They had absolutely nothing. I looked at many tiny dirt shacks where entire families lived, as we walked from the house to the church. I fought back tears.

When Tammy and I entered the church, we saw our friends seated up in the front, who motioned for us to join them. They sat on large chairs, including arm rests, with purple and white cloths draped over the chairs. My friends looked like royalty sitting on their thrones, while the congregation sat on small wooden benches. I did not want to sit on those throne-like chairs, but it would have been insulting if I did not. I felt ridiculous.

My friends stood to hug me. Jim was quite surprised to see me since he heard that Brian was not coming, and he wondered how I got here; I told him by taxi, and he laughed in surprised delight. Jim proceeded to introduce me to the congregation and invited me to say something. The Kenyan people on this mountain hung on every word spoken and loved to be in church to worship. It was a great joy to be a part of their worship service, even though it lasted over four hours! Jim and Dana both spoke, Karmen played her guitar and sang, and Tammy spoke through tears. Finally, the service ended and the congregation left to eat lunch, while we went back to the house to rest and to eat together.

Dana began to cook pasta with cheese sauce, and there was a chocolate cake in the oven! I was expecting peanut butter sandwiches, which Jim said we would probably eat. I had felt sorry for my friends, who I found were eating and living far better than I was.... They also brought out the Rice Krispie treats they made last night. Later that evening, they said they would be going to someone's home for a complete chicken dinner. I laughed and said I felt like taking my treats back home, though of course I did not, and we all enjoyed each other's company for the next couple of hours. It is funny how when you are deprived of something so simple as your usual diet, how important food can become; surely that must be true for hungry people with nothing to eat.

The church service was set to resume in two hours, which would be 4:00 p.m., but Jim told me I should probably head back to Kitale since it looked like it was going to rain and the dirt roads would never allow the taxi driver's car to make it down the mountain once the rain began. Not wanting to get stuck in the mud in the middle of a mountain, and knowing I had to teach the next day, I told my friends that I had a great day, hugged them all, and Mrs. Bill and I got back into the small car to go back to Kitale. Our taxi driver, Francis, thought we made a wise decision as well. On our way back to town, Francis stopped a young boy walking along the road and asked him to cut us some sugar cane. Francis knew that I had never tasted sugar cane, and he and Mrs. Bill showed me how to suck the juice out of it and enjoy the sweetness, while we listened to praise and worship music on the tape player in the car. I looked down from the mountain onto the beautiful Kenyan fields. I was in Africa, and I loved it.

Back to Kitale

After thanking Francis and Mrs. Bill, I went into my cottage to rest and prepare for the next day's teaching. It was 8:45 p.m.; suddenly, the power went out. It was pitch black. I could not see a thing. I began to feel my way around the cottage to the bedroom where I had a tiny battery operated travel alarm clock. The clock had a blue light that shown when you pressed a button to display the time, and it gave me just enough light to locate the small flashlight my dad had the good sense to pack for me. There were also matches and candles in each room of the cottage for such a time as this. I could not believe how dark it was in Kenya. There was not one light on in the entire compound. All of the security lights were out as well, and I was a bit frightened. I finally found some lanterns and candles to shine some light in my cottage. Because the light was so dim, I was unable to study my lessons, so I proceeded to get ready for bed. I prayed.

Not having light greatly inhibited so much that I needed to do, such as study and prepare for my work, and I hoped this interruption of electricity would not last for long. Shortly after I began praying, the lights came back on and once again, I felt safe; thank you Jesus. I realized there was only true safety in the arms of my Savior.

The following day would be the last full day of class, then a review day, and the Final Exam. The work at the seminary was long and hard, but now that it was coming to an end, I felt sad. I came to really love these students and everyone I met at the seminary. After class, I spoke with Bill, the Director of the seminary, and he asked me if I could return the following year to teach again. I responded with delight, and told him I would like to bring my son Joshua with me, in order for him to share in this wonderful experience as well. We were both excited.

The next day when I got to class, I told my students that I planned on returning to teach again in a year. They applauded and laughed and were so happy, but they asked if I would teach a different subject so that I would have them as students again. I promised I would ask, and that I would be honored. It was our last class together, and my students presented me with several beautiful gifts, to which I was most amazed. The love and generosity of my students will never cease to amaze me.

Ponderings

As I sat alone in my cottage the last night in the seminary compound, I pondered full-time mission work. I gained a new respect for Bill, for Jim and Henny, for Brian and Heather, and for all full-time missionaries. Going on a short-term mission trip was easy; it was an adventure, filled with excitement, with the opportunity to meet new people, to see new things, to experience different cultures, and it felt like a "working" vacation. But after the excitement and the newness wears down and missionaries settle into a strange place where they are not always understood (nor understand others), when they willingly give up their homes, comforts, luxuries, conveniences, favorite foods, etc., life could be quite difficult and isolating. I believe missionaries understand, probably better than most Christians, what Scripture means when Jesus said:

"Anyone who follows Me cannot be My disciple unless he loves Me more than his father and mother, wife and children, brothers and sisters, yes and his own life also. And whoever does not bear his own cross and follow Me, cannot be My disciple" (Luke 14:26-27 DNT).

I thought about the hours of earnest prayers that I heard from my students from the prayer room when I jogged past it each morning in the compound while I too prayed as I ran. My prayers though, were not like theirs, which were so full of deep longings, emotions and great faith. They needed so much, they had so little, but they lived out their faith in such a greater capacity than did I. My ponderings were aborted when I remembered that the next morning my American friends from Mt. Elgon would be coming to pick me up so we could all spend a couple of days together to relax and to go on an African safari.

An African Paradise

The van pulled up to my cottage carrying Jim, Tammy, Dana and Karmen from the mountain. They were tired from their work, as was I, but, like me, they were also sad to leave the people they too came to love. I quickly showed them around my cottage and the seminary, said some tearful good byes to my students while we had our last cup of chai together, and I promised them, Lord willing, to see them next year. We boarded the van and off we went.

After a few hours, we arrived at Lake Baringo. The grounds were beautiful, filled with all varieties of trees and colorful flowers. There was a path in the tall grass that led down to the lake where crocodiles sunned themselves on rocks and hippos stayed cool in the water. Birds of all sizes and colors swarmed the area and flew in spectacular displays while we sat by the swimming pool and drank chai. Tammy and I shared a room at the lodge that amazed us both with its charm and African decor. We unpacked and went to the lodge dining area for a nice buffet dinner, which included a wonderful variety of foods.

Boat rides were offered each morning to go out on the lake and see the crocodiles and hippos up close, which we all wanted to do. The hotel staff warned us though only to take a boat ride offered by the lodge, and not to accept a ride from the "locals" who would ask us to go with them in their "unauthorized" boats which were considered unsafe, and of which the lodge would not guarantee our safety.

Later that day, we were indeed approached by the "locals" to take a boat ride with them, who offered a cheaper price from the lodge rates, and they also offered to take us out before dawn in order to watch the sun rise from the middle of the lake. Because of the danger of the hippos while it was still dark, the lodge boats would not begin taking visitors out until after the sun came up. Hippos spend their days in the water to keep cool, but at night, they come out to eat grass. Hippos kill more people in Kenya than any other animal, so no one at this lodge was allowed to roam the grounds at night or walk down to the lake.

The cheap offer of an adventure to go out while still dark sounded too tempting for us, so we accepted and agreed to meet them down by the lake at 6:00 a.m. Tammy, however, decided that after two weeks in Kenya, safely coming through the travels and dangers already encountered, she did not want to risk this "adventure" and decided she would sleep in. The rest of us, however, were excited.

The guards that watched the grounds at night warned us not to leave our rooms after dark because of the hippos, which would roam around the lodge grounds in front of our rooms to eat the tall grass. The staff at the lodge said that if visitors want to see the hippos, they needed to inform the night watchmen which room they were in, and a guard would knock on the guests' door to take them out to see these large and dangerous animals. We were allowed to sit outside of our rooms though to try and see the hippos, but we could not wander the grounds. The four of us sat, and watched, and waited, but the hippos never came. We were all tired, so we gave our room numbers to the guards and went to bed. The guards, however, never came to any of our rooms, so we did not see any hippos that night. I set my alarm clock for 5:00 a.m. and fell asleep anxious for the morning, looking forward to our sunrise boat ride.

Crazy Adventures

When my alarm went off the next morning, I asked Tammy once again if she wanted to join us, but she declined, told me we were crazy, and went back to sleep. I was excited, got ready, and went outside to meet Jim, Dana and Karmen. It was pitch black outside. Kenyan nights are dark, and there are no street lights or path lights as there are in American lodges. Dana and I brought small flashlights to help us navigate our way down the path to the lake. We had about a half mile walk to the lake, which felt like ten miles; it was frightening. We spoke about the warnings of taking the "unauthorized" boats that were deemed unsafe. We spoke about the tall grass all around us; what if there were hippos still out eating, who could see us, but we could not see them? In good humor, Jim began to recite his Last Will to his "Dear wife Henny," while Dana and I figured out that we were only saving about fifty cents each by riding with the "locals" while we put our lives in jeopardy. We were all joking around, but deep inside, I think we were all scared. We also prayed together on our walk to the lake.

We made it to the shore of beautiful Lake Baringo, in a frightening walk that felt like it took hours, though it was just a few minutes, to our "unauthorized" boat and the "local" who was waiting for us. We got in his tiny hand-made canoe that we were sure would tip or be knocked over by a hippo, and set out to the middle of the lake to watch the sun rise over the African mountains. It was beautiful. We saw many hippos and crocodiles, though they (thankfully) basically ignored us. Our guide stopped several times to point out some beautiful eagles in the trees along the bank. He then made a call to the eagles, which flew over to him, and he threw a fish in the air for one of the eagles to catch. He repeated this scene several times. We were all amazed and enjoyed ourselves immensely. Our fears disappeared, and we spoke of our love for Africa and its beauty.

The Safari

After our adventure out on the lake, we cleaned up, ate breakfast, packed our luggage and headed off to our next destination; the African Safari. We drove for a few more hours with the opportunity to see more of this beautiful land of Kenya, and arrived at another African paradise known as Nakuru Game Park. Again, Tammy and I shared a room, and again, we were amazed at the beauty of the lodge and of everything in the room. We unpacked, had something to eat, and got ready for an Africa safari! We rode in a Toyota mini-van with a roof that opened up, which enabled us to stand and look out at the African plains and to get a closer view of the animals. Our driver took us out as dusk was approaching. The animals come out to hunt, to feed, and to graze in the evenings and in the early mornings, which is when people go out to try to see them. Tourists are not allowed to go out after dark for their own safety, and cannot leave the vehicle. However, we still had several hours of daylight and we were anxious to see the animals.

As we drove through the plains, Dana said with a huge smile, "We're in Africa!" The excitement hit us all as we shared in that smile. We drove through the beauty of Kenya and saw lions, water buffalo, zebras, giraffes, gazelles, rhinoceros, baboons, wart hogs, a leopard, and the sheer beauty of the African trees and plains. Since it was becoming dark, our driver headed back to the lodge, where we had a good night's sleep. Excitedly, we went out again in the early morning to see the animals as the sun rose over the African plains. Once again, we had a spectacular time.

While my bucket list dream was to go on an African safari, this recent adventure seemed to diminish in comparison to the people I met. The part of this African trip that was most meaningful to me were my students, their desire to learn and to serve God, the faith I witnessed in them, and the commitment to God that these Kenyan people lived with on a daily basis. My life was changed; my faith was challenged. I was ready to go home and share this amazing experience, and to return next year for more.

Kenya remained a priority on my bucket list.

KENYA

"We think within the confines of our language, which is quite different from culture to culture."

3

RETURNING TO KENYA

Memories and Hopes

Where could I begin? I had so many stories to tell, so many pictures to show of my African trip, and I was so excited about everything! I was anxious to show my son the pictures I had taken, and I was surprised to see that most of the photos were of the people–my students at the seminary and friends I had made. While I did have quite a few photos of the safari, the animal pictures were the minority; I knew at that moment what was special to me about Kenya and why I wanted to return: it was the people!

Joshua looked at the photos, listened to my stories, and appeared excited (well, at least pretty interested). I spoke about Kenya constantly, which he reminded me of often. "He needs to go," I thought, "so he will understand my enthusiasm." I had an idea: he would be graduating from college that year, and for his graduation gift, I would buy him a plane ticket to Kenya. I began to plan, and to continue to talk about Africa.

Time passed, and I continued to plan, to work hard for our two plane tickets, and I was anxious for Joshua to graduate college. He worked hard in college, earned good grades, and I knew he was thankful to complete the work in order to begin the next chapter of life. His college career came to a close with a huge party at our church gym, which our pastor was gracious enough to allow us to use. Joshua received a generous amount of money in gifts. To my amazement, because he is so thoughtful, he spent the graduation money on some beautiful diamond earrings for me in appreciation for paying for his college. What a surprise! However, I now had a surprise for Joshua: his plane ticket to Kenya.

The Beginning of the Journey

Since I had shown my son the many places I had traveled in my photographs of Kenya, which peaked his interest, I thought I should take him to those same places so that he could experience them for himself. We began our journey with a layover in London, which enabled us to tour the city, and which we both found quite interesting. The layover was also a good way to break up the exhausting flight from Chicago to Nairobi. After a long day of touring London, we returned to the airport, boarded the plane, and settled in for the final part of our travels. Next, we would be in Kenya.

We arrived at the hot Nairobi airport, found our luggage, went through customs, and were greeted by our driver Francis, who would take us to the Mennonite Guest house for a couple of nights. This guesthouse was a beautiful, welcoming place to stay, with communal dining, hosted by an American missionary couple who now called Nairobi their home. The yard was beautifully landscaped, filled with trees, bushes, and exotic, colorful flowers that reminded us of the beauty we saw in Hawaii. We were in Africa.

The next day, Joshua met a young man from Rwanda, whose family had been brutally murdered in the ethnic cleansing that recently occurred in that country. With unbelief, my son listened to this young man's heart-breaking story, and of how he came to live at this guesthouse through the compassionate love of Jesus displayed in this missionary couple. Neither my son nor I had ever heard a story of such gruesomeness and sorrow as we heard from this Rwandan man. Joshua experienced his first discomfort of Kenya, amidst the natural beauty which surrounded us. Kenya was to be a land of great sorrow, but also a land of great love and hope.

Kitale

After coffee and a wonderful breakfast, where we had the chance to meet other travelers, Francis picked us up to take us to our destination of Kitale. The drive was almost eight hours long through mostly dusty, pothole-filled roads that only the best of drivers could navigate. The joke in Kenya is that drunk drivers drive straight! Francis was indeed an excellent driver, and also quite friendly. He drove past some beautiful sights and stopped at places where he assumed we would want to see, from the Great Rift Valley to souvenir shops at the equator. We enjoyed the scenery. Along the way, we also saw many zebras, baboons and other wildlife that one would normally not see when driving through the States, and certainly not in the Chicago area!

That evening, we arrived at the seminary compound where we would be living for the next two weeks. Francis brought us to the same cottage where I stayed the previous year, which was clean and simple. The floors and walls were painted concrete, and there was a wicker living room set, with furniture that most Americans use for their screened porches or Florida rooms. The cottage had three bedrooms and two bathrooms, plus a small kitchen, which accommodated us just fine. We each chose a bedroom, unpacked, and settled in. We then prepared ourselves for the following day to begin teaching. I was slightly nervous, but I also knew that my students would immediately put me at ease. Joshua was to sit in with me on the class this year and assist as needed, and if he chose to return, he would get his own classroom the next year (which is precisely what happened the following year). Joshua seemed excited, though tired, and after looking around the compound, we went to our rooms for a good sleep. The following morning, our work and the adventure would begin.

The Classroom

Because I loved my students so much from my first year in Kenya, I asked the seminary if I could teach a different course the following year, to the same group of students, to which the administration agreed. I had taken pictures of each of the students the previous year, so the faces were familiar to Joshua when he met the class. The previous year, when my students had learned that I had a son, they all expected me to return with him, so there was great excitement amongst all of them when we both walked into the classroom. We were greeted with huge smiles and handshakes as the introductions began. It was a strange feeling, but I felt like I had just returned home to my family.

Class began, and Joshua observed and also spoke when he was needed. After several hours, the classroom work was broken up by mid-morning tea, which was an informal time when my students and I could reconnect, and where they also began to know my son whom I had spoken about the previous year. Another way we became better acquainted with our students was in the opportunity to eat lunch with them each day. We all found this time of eating together to be a wonderful time of fellowship. Joshua loves to tell stories, so sometimes after lunch, he and the students would sit on the grass in the compound and share life through stories. We are truly one when we know Jesus and have the same Heavenly Father.

The workday was long, both for teachers and the students, though the students paid attention and understood the assignments well. Most of the students were the same age as Joshua, or only a few years older, and they were pastors or Christian leaders in their communities. However, in rural, poverty-stricken Kenya, these men and women were not educated and trained in their roles, so this seminary training was important to ensure proper teaching of the Scriptures in the local churches. The students were hungry for knowledge and eager to learn. The next ten days consisted of teaching, grading homework at night, and discovering Kenya and the wonderful people who live there. My son seemed to fit right in, and he and the students bonded quickly, just as I had bonded with them the previous year.

Culture and Frisbees

Most of the students traveled from all across Kenya to attend this seminary at a great sacrifice of time and money. Therefore, the classes were taught as "intensives," which means a full course is covered in ten days. In order to accomplish this task, the days are long, about ten hours of teaching, reading, writing and completing assignments. Consequently, the students sit for most of the day. The previous year, as I considered the sedentary days of study, I thought it would be fun to bring some Frisbees to throw around in the large, open field of the compound; so this year, I packed several Frisbees in my luggage.

When the class room day ended that first evening, Joshua brought out the Frisbees. We threw a Frisbee back and forth to each other as the students observed. None of the students had ever seen a Frisbee, and they asked us what these "plates" were that we threw back and forth to one another. Of course, we asked them to join us, which they did with great enthusiasm.

One of the best Frisbee players was Jackson, of the Pokot tribe. Jackson was intrigued by the Frisbee, and asked Joshua to teach him to throw it. With only a couple of throws, Jackson whipped that Frisbee through the air with strength and accuracy which amazed and confounded both Joshua and me. Jackson became known as "the Frisbee Master" which he delighted in as much as we delighted in watching him play. This simple pastime of throwing around Frisbees became another bonding experience for us, especially for my son and Jackson, who became fast friends. Jackson's life would soon have a powerful impact on Joshua as they learned more about one another. Their relationship basically began through a simple activity of Frisbee, which Americans play often, but which was such fun, excitement and wonder to these Kenyan men and women.

As the students quickly learned to throw and catch a Frisbee, Joshua and I quickly learned that there were indeed many cultural differences and barriers between people from either side of the ocean. People are so much alike in many ways, yet various cultures do indeed have their differences, which need to be recognized, respected, and worked through with mutual love and respect.

One cultural difference is in the way men display friendship in Kenya; they hold hands. Walking through the compound one day, I noticed Jackson take an American man's hand. In America, holding hands with someone of the same sex implied a homosexual relationship. This American man, somewhat repulsed by this unknown display of affection, snatched his hand away in horror! Jackson was hurt and embarrassed. This simple cultural difference made a huge impact on the relationship between two friends, simply for lack of understanding. I explained to this man that hand holding among men was perfectly normal in this culture, and he apologized to Jackson and explained the misunderstanding. Though uncomfortable, I watched several American men as they walked through the compound holding hands with their new Kenyan friends. After all, we were in Africa!

Language proved to be another cultural barrier. While the students at the seminary all spoke, read, and wrote in English, there were phrases and words that differed, which sometimes created problems. There were many phrases that Americans use that are unfamiliar to Kenyans, and also words, phrases and even pronunciations that differ so vastly from each culture that we did not understand one another. When I was teaching Church History, I used the word, *"Renaissance."* My students had no idea what I was talking about, not because they were unfamiliar with that period of time, but because of the way that I pronounced the word, which was much different from the way they pronounced it. After many laughs, I was finally able to continue with my lesson. Indeed, there are cultural differences, and I discovered that our differences stem primarily from the uses of language.

We think within the confines of our language, which is quite different from culture to culture. While some of these cultural differences we found humorous and laughed at together, there were other differences that were not funny and did not have that light-hearted effect, such as the hand-holding among male friends, and other differences that we will discover later.

Jackson's Poverty

Jackson, the Frisbee Master, was a skinny, quiet, gentle man from the Pokot tribe of Kenya. The Pokot's remember, are poor, nomadic people who live by raiding villages and stealing cattle. Before becoming a Christian, the Pokot's way of life was normal for Jackson. It was difficult for Joshua and me to believe that such a gentle, quiet man like Jackson once lived that type of life, raiding cattle. Jackson had been basically homeless, but after attending this seminary and learning to read and write more proficiently, he got a job and began a much better life than he had ever known. Jackson was an incredibly intelligent man, but he was never given the opportunities to utilize his intelligence. Joshua was quite impressed with Jackson's intellect, his kindness, and his faith.

One Saturday after class, Jackson was anxious to show Joshua and me his new home, of which he was rather proud. We agreed to take this journey with our friend to see his home. We walked through garbage-filled, crowded dirt roads to a mud and dung building consisting of about seven "apartments" in a row, with a communal out-house in back. Jackson took us to the door of one of these apartments and welcomed us into his home. We looked around at the one room, which consisted of a wooden table with two wooden chairs and a twin bed. There were no windows. There was no electricity. There was no light. There was no water, sink, or toilet. There was no stove. The walls and floor were mud. We left the door ajar for some light.

Jackson smiled and pulled out the chairs for us to sit. Joshua glanced at me and then smiled at Jackson, and said, "Wow Jackson, this is great!" Jackson gave a proud smile in return. It was difficult to believe that this was an improvement to the life he once lived.

We sat and talked for a while, and then Jackson wanted to show us the rest of this area where he lived. Jackson locked the large wooden door to his apartment and walked with us to the end of this mud building to a small empty room which had a water pump. The people who lived there would bring their bucket and towel to this small room to take their bath at the water pump. There was usually a small fire burning next to this "bathroom" to warm up the water before bathing. I thought of my wonderful clean shower back home which I take for granted each day. I wondered if Jackson could even imagine what a typical American shower was like.

Jackson had a couple of Kenyan shillings (Kenyan currency), and he wanted to treat us to some chai, as a thank you for traveling with him to see his home. We appreciated Jackson's' gratitude and his desire to express his friendship, and we knew that we would insult him if we did not allow him to buy our chai; with disbelief, and with the little bit of money Jackson had, we enjoyed our chai together in a small café. We were truly feeling a great chasm between cultures. Not knowing where his next shilling would come from, Jackson shared the last of what he had on his friends because he loved us and because he trusted Jesus to provide for him. In amazement, Joshua asked Jackson how he lives, since his faith seemed so strong, but resources were so few. Jackson gave a simple answer; "I live by the grace of God." Jackson scribbled that message down for Joshua on a small piece of notebook paper, which he kept in his pocket. To this day, my son has that note framed and hung in his home as a reminder of true Christianity.

A Typical Rural Kenyan Home

We had another student named Fred who also wanted to take us to his home. Fred said he taught driving to local people, and he could therefore get a car and take us to see his home on Sunday after church. We agreed to go. Bill, the Director of the seminary, warned us not to take any public transportation, since the vans (called *mutatus)*, were all overcrowded, they were not equipped with seat belts, and all far exceeded a safe speed limit. We assured Bill that we would be traveling by car, so he told us it would be alright to go.

Fred said he would meet us at the seminary with his car, and drive us to his home. However, when Fred came to the seminary, he did not have a car, and he asked us to walk into town with him. We thought that perhaps we needed to go to some driving school to pick up the car. Instead, we waited on the mud street for the *mutatu* to pick us up, which was the fast, dangerous, over-crowded minivan we were told not to take! Though surprised, we remained silent, paid our shillings, and boarded the van so we would not hurt Fred's feelings. We later learned that Fred was unable to obtain a car for the day as he had previously thought.

Joshua is tall and muscular, and larger than most Kenyan men, so he was told to sit up front with the driver where there was more room. Fred and I squeezed ourselves in between far too many people, including a woman holding a large, live rooster. The van quickly picked up speed, and I began to understand why Bill did not want us to ride this death trap. With each stop, I assumed people would be getting off as the others got on, but they did not; more and more people simply pushed their way in, some even hanging on the outside of the van for their ride! I prayed, as I tried to appear calm and unconcerned. We finally reached our stop, got out of the *mutatu*, and stretched our legs. I was thankful to still be alive, as many people die each day in these vans from accidents.

Fred assured us that his house was, "Just right over there" as we walked for miles, while he continued to say, "It's just right over there." I began to wonder just how many more "just right over there" statements there were! We walked probably a mile or more, and I admit I was somewhat nervous. Joshua and I were the only light-skinned, non-African people in this rural area, and several men began to follow us. Fortunately, my son is a tall, strong, muscular man, so I did not think too many shorter, skinny African men might consider taking him on. Joshua noticed some men following us, clenched his fists, and strode with confidence; they soon disappeared.

We finally reached the "just right over there" and arrived at Fred's house. His wife and small children came to welcome us with warm greetings. Fred and his family lived in a mud and dung house. The house was small and dark. Fred's wife offered us some water, but we politely declined, knowing our American stomachs would probably get quite sick drinking their water, since we only drank bottled water while in Kenya. Fred was proud of his house, which he built with his own hands, and he felt like a good provider for his family (which indeed he was).

We sat and visited for a while until the rains came. When Fred's wife saw the rain, she quickly gathered buckets and placed them outside so she could collect the rain water, since the house had no plumbing. She cooked on an open fire, since there was no electricity and no lights in the house. There was no plumbing of any kind, and they used an outhouse near the back of their home that Fred built for their bathroom.

The lives of Fred and his family appeared difficult without any modern conveniences. I thought of how simple tasks such as bathing, laundry, and cooking would consume a large portion of their day, and how dark it must be for them at night without any lights. I had no idea how far Fred's wife would have to walk for firewood to cook, since we walked far to the house, without a large forest nearby. Not feeling completely safe walking with both my son and Fred, I wondered how safe Fred's wife felt going for firewood each day so she could cook for her family.

As I pondered all of these difficulties, I was quite thankful to be an American with all of our modern conveniences. My life was far easier than the lives of Fred and his family, and the many other rural Kenyans who lived in this same manner. Would their lives always be this difficult? In sadness, I sat in this dark home as I listened to the rain, and tried to pay attention to the conversation going on around me, despite the difficult circumstance of their life that surrounded me. When the rains slowed down, we walked back to the "bus stop" to catch the *mutatu* back to Kitale. I hoped Bill, the seminary director, would not ask about our mode of transport.

Kenyan Hospitality

The Bible speaks a great deal about the importance of hospitality, which the Kenyans practice far better than most Americans. Each evening, one of the seminary staff was scheduled to pick up any Americans who were working at the seminary, and take them to their home for dinner. This wonderful act of hospitality enabled us to get to know not only the people, but also the local customs and Kenyan culture. I looked forward to the 6:00 pick up from a different family each night, to see where we would be going, whose home we would visit, and who we would get to know that evening. We met some truly amazing people, whose kindness and warmth is beyond comparison. The Kenyan staff people did not know us at all, yet they prepared wonderful meals for us and welcomed us into their homes as if we had been friends for years, which is how we felt.

One family, the Maiyo's, lived in America for several years where Kibii Maiyo did his graduate studies in theology. I had met Kibii the previous year in Kenya, and he knew that being from Chicago, Joshua and I loved pizza. Kibii and Esther Maiyo were two of the kindest people I have ever met, and they have a daughter named Chepchumba, who made us pizza for our evening meal. Though the pizza was much different than we were accustomed to eating, we were humbled by the consideration of this family in preparing pizzas for some visiting

Chicago Americans. We had a wonderful time of fellowship in their home. After the "American" meal, Kibii brought out song books from his church and we all sang together and then drank our chai. Before driving us back to our cottage, we had prayer together and looked forward to returning to their home again. To this day, we remain good friends with Kibii and his family.

On another evening, Joshua and I were picked up by a man named Nathan Chesang, who served as the Chairman of the Board of the seminary where we taught. Nathan's face shone with the love of Jesus, and he wore a huge smile almost all of the time. He spoke quickly, with a strong Kenyan accent, and I had difficulty understanding him. Nathan was full of light and laughter, and I could sense the Holy Spirit in his words, even when I was unsure of what he was saying. I had never met a man with such a strong presence of Jesus before; he was truly unique. His wife Josephine prepared a huge, wonderful meal for us as we began to get acquainted. Smiles, laughter and joy were in abundance, and I wanted to spend more time around this man. Surely, I could learn much from Nathan. I had no idea that this was only the beginning of our friendship.

Servant hood and Light Development Foundation

Seminary classes were in session on Saturday's until noon, at which point those students who were able, could go home for the remainder of the weekend. Nathan picked up Joshua and me after class to show us another ministry that he was involved in as the country director, called SELIDEF, which the local people understand to mean "Servant hood and Light Development Foundation".

SELIDEF was in its infancy, with a building under construction for its headquarters in Kitale, and the vision was just beginning for all this ministry would encompass. Nathan explained this ministry's focus: electricity/light, cooking stoves and clean water for rural Kenya, along with evangelizing though practical ways of helping people to live better lives, and also through classes, Bible teachings, and through the Jesus film that would be played at the centers where people would congregate. Circular light bulbs would be sold for a small fee to people to take to their homes, including the battery that would power the light, and also small two-burner cooking stoves that resembled Coleman camping stoves. I had one of these stoves in my cottage at the seminary, and I liked it. The light bulbs ran off of batteries that would last for about one month. When the month was over, the rural Kenyans could come to the center in their area and get new batteries, which were recharged for continuous use. The cooking stoves ran off of propane tanks that also lasted about a month, and could be refilled for another month's use.

The people of the villages that SELIDEF would serve would walk or ride bicycles to come to their particular center. There were also plans for classes and trainings on the Christian faith to be held in the communication centers at the SELIDEF areas. Nathan also hoped that bore holes would be drilled so these rural areas would have access to clean water. I thought about Fred's wife running outside with buckets to catch the rain water when we sat in their house. Another vision Nathan had for these centers, was to have an orphanage at each site to provide housing and care for the many AIDS orphans throughout Africa. SELIDEF appeared to truly be an amazing and much needed ministry in rural Kenya, and I was excited.

Stoves

There were several reasons for the idea of cooking stoves. Much of Africa has been damaged by the continuous deforestation that has occurred over the years, since people use wood to cook. Like Fred's wife, the women have to walk many miles into the forest each day to chop down trees and branches and carry back heavy bundles of wood to begin preparing meals. Environmentally, this process of cutting down so many trees is destroying Africa. The long walks into the woods are time consuming, they involve heavy work, and they are not always safe, as women have to walk further and further to find more wood. Once the woman does finally return home, there are health and safety risks for the family, and especially for the children. With open fires burning in the homes, small children have sometimes fallen into the fires and suffered severe burns. The smoke is also unhealthy, which people breathe in for hours and consequently suffer from various diseases and respiratory problems due to smoke inhalation. Meal preparation is also quite time-consuming, since walking to gather the wood, making fires, and cooking can take almost all day in what would take someone in a modern kitchen only minutes to prepare.

Electricity

The reasoning for the light bulbs was also multi-faceted. The rural school children cannot study after nightfall when Kenya gets pitch black. The small paraffin lamps or candles that families use do not project enough light for reading, which limits the time children can do homework and learn. I knew of this problem by experience whenever my cottage lost power and I wanted to study or prepare my lessons for the following day, but could not, due to the dim light of candles and lanterns. Because of this limitation of light, the rural children cannot compete with children in the cities who have access to electricity; therefore, they do not do as well in school. Women can also get some house work done in the evenings, and families can spend more time together in activities when there is light in the home. SELIDEF therefore, sought to improve the lives of rural Kenyans educationally, environmentally, and by improving their health. The hope was also that many Kenyans, who, prior to SELIDEF were not Christians, would come to know Jesus because they could see a God who cares about their lives. Making tangible improvements in the lives of people, in addition to preaching the Gospel, is how others see Jesus. Most of us are familiar with the famous quote of Saint Francis of Assisi who said, *"Preach the Gospel at all times; when necessary, use words."*

Television

The Jesus film was also going to be played at these centers so that people could hear and see the Gospel, and they would naturally be interested since they had never seen a television before. These rural Kenyans would have the opportunity to hear the Gospel story told, and hear Jesus speak in their native language, since the film was translated into Swahili. (Years later, I was told that many people, came to accept Jesus as their Savior through this film, which is a wonderful evangelistic tool used throughout the world).

Orphanages

Nathan then showed us the area where SELIDEF hoped to build an orphanage, since there are so many AIDS orphans in Kenya. Joshua and I had seen many street children begging for food, which broke our hearts. When Nathan spoke about the vision for the orphanages at each site, my heart filled with a plethora of emotions and I began to cry. Joshua said to Nathan, "Look, my mom is crying!" Nathan looked at me with quiet amazement, as I dried my tears, unsure of why they even flowed. Perhaps someday I would understand.

Trees

Trees had just begun to be planted at the main headquarters in Kitale, to represent the end of deforestation in this country through SELIDEF. Nathan wanted us to plant our trees. It began to rain, so some employees of SELIDEF came out with umbrellas which they held over us as we dug the holes and planted the trees. I felt a special connection to SELIDEF that I hoped would last a life time. I planted a tree at the corner of the plot of land in this small new forest. I felt grounded here as I planted my tree, which was only the beginning of my statement for growth and life between American Christians and Kenya. We had no idea what lay ahead, but there were plenty of hopes, tears and laughter.

Nathan

I began to know Nathan through this amazing work with SELIDEF, and I saw a man of unusual faith and strength. He was a visionary who believed in a God who does great things, and who can use anyone, including himself. Nathan grew up poor in a mud hut in rural Mt. Elgon in Kenya, where my American friends Tammy, Jim, Dana and Karmen worked that first year I came to Africa. When Nathan left his family home, he worked as a fruit salesman, selling mainly pineapples and bananas on the street market. Realizing that he would always live in dire poverty doing this type of work, he learned to weld and began working as a welder. Since all of the doors and windows in Kenya have bars across them, there appeared to be plenty of work for a welder. After some experience in this trade, Nathan decided to start his own welding shop and started a small business of his own, which became more profitable. Nathan was now married and had a wife and child to support, with two more children who would eventually also be born to him and his wife Josephine.

Nathan did not have a formal education, but he was a man of unusual insight and wisdom, which I think other people could readily see. One man observed Nathan and asked him to work for him selling insurance. Nathan had absolutely no idea about, or knowledge of, the insurance business; but, this man trained him for only two hours, and Nathan became an insurance agent! Today, he is widely sought after in Kenya as a trusted and respected insurance agent. Nathan had also been told by a friend to buy some stock (again, which Nathan knew nothing about); however, years later his investment proved extremely lucrative.

Nathan's life quickly began to change. He was asked to be the Chairman of the Board of Directors for the seminary where I taught annually in Kenya, and he was also the country Director of this new SELIDEF ministry that I had the opportunity to watch evolve. Eventually, I would spend more time with Nathan and his family during the next four years as I made my annual trip to Kenya to teach. Little did I know that my Kenyan friends, especially Nathan, would change my life.

Going Home

Joshua and I completed our classes, and headed out to enjoy some of the Kenyan scenery, and to go on safari. I wanted to take him to the same places I had been to the year before, to see the animals and to complete our African trip. We had several hours in the car to get to our destinations, and went through times of silence and quiet reflection, and times of conversation about the beauty of the land. At times, we also spoke about many of the new experiences that we each had. It was sad leaving our new friends, and we spoke about how sad it was seeing the level of poverty in which they lived. Seeing Third World poverty for oneself, living among it, rather than viewing it through a television screen or in magazine pages, and becoming friends with people who live in such desperate ways takes a great emotional toll. I was worn down emotionally; I wondered if my son was as well. My heart became heavy, but I knew I would be back, and that life never stays the same.

The Real Kenya

Most people I know come to Kenya to see the beauty of the land, to go on a safari, and to see the big game: lions, elephants, rhinos, hippos, giraffes, etc. While these things are an important, beautiful and prevalent aspect of Kenya, the real Kenya for me was the people.

For the next four years I returned to Kenya to teach at the seminary, to visit my friends, and to see Nathan and his family, whom I dearly loved. Seeing Nathan was my annual "spiritual tune-up." His faith and his joy in the Lord were unlike anything I had ever experienced. Nathan has two sayings that stuck into my heart: "God is very organized," and "Have fun with Jesus." Nathan knew that a life lived in obedience and surrender to Jesus brought joy unspeakable, and changed his life in drastic ways that no one could ever imagine. Nathan went from a fruit salesman to the Chairman of the Board of a seminary and the Country Director of a growing ministry headed by some powerful, rich Americans who had great respect and admiration for this wise, though uneducated man. People knew there was something special about Nathan, and I wanted to be around him in order to learn to have his faith, his joy, and his enthusiasm for Jesus.

Too often, missionaries think they come to a country such as Kenya to help and teach the Kenyans; that is what I initially thought. However, I soon learned the opposite; the reality is that I came to Kenya to be taught and to learn how to live with total and complete dependency on God, as many of my Kenyan friends live. My Kenyan students and friends taught me far more than I ever taught them.

I returned to Kenya four more times looking forward to seeing my students, my many friends such as Kibii and his family and Nebert and his wife, spending time with Nathan and his family, and sharing meals with them in their homes. Kenya was feeling like my second home, and I loved hearing my friends say to me, "Welcome home," as they greeted me with a big hug each time I returned. I was indeed home. I was in Africa.

Disappointment

After traveling to Kenya annually for six years, I was unable to return for the next four years due to many life changes, moves, deaths, trials, and difficulties. Because of this time lapse, I did not remain in touch with Nathan and my other Kenyan friends as I would have otherwise desired. One reason for the lack of communication stemmed from a huge hurt and disappointment which came from Kenya. Because I loved Kenya as I did, I prayed about going to teach at the seminary in Kitale full time and to live in Kenya for a one to three year term. I was previously asked if I would consider teaching full time by several staff members at the seminary, as well as by all of my students, and I thought this was the time. I contacted the founder and president of the seminary, went through all the proper channels, and began planning for my life in Kenya. A full psychiatric exam was also administered to determine if I would be able to live overseas; the results were positive. I was excited. I began telling friends and family that I would be moving to Kenya! God was surely giving me the desires of my heart–at last.

Shortly before going to bed one night, I looked at my emails, and found one from Pete, the new Director of the seminary in Kitale where I was planning to work. Tears filled my eyes as I began to read. For no apparent reason, and with no explanation, I was told I could not come out full time to teach, but that I was welcomed to come out for a couple of weeks as I had been doing thus far. My heart sank to my toes. My stomach churned. I was devastated, hurt and confused. What happened? What was the explanation for this? I cried myself to sleep that night, I prayed, and I wondered why God took away my dream. Without any explanation, I quietly removed myself from Kenya for a while, and remained at a distance to soften the blow.

Back in Communication

Periodically I would be in touch with my friends from Kenya through email, though not on a regular basis. I still communicated with Kibii, who remains a good friend, and with Nebert, who is also a dear friend to this day. Eventually, Nathan and I resumed contact, and I told him about what happened concerning my desire to come out to live in Kenya, and how that was suddenly aborted. Nathan told me that my pain was probably for the best right now, and he began to tell me that there were some serious problems concerning him, the seminary, and deep pain and disappointments that he was also going through, though he was quite vague. Nathan was no longer with the seminary, nor was he the Chairman of the Board, and he was struggling to keep SELIDEF going since all of the American support was stopped. The American supporters pulled out from SELIDEF and away from Nathan. I could not understand what was happening, but life in Kenya, and specifically for Nathan, was unraveling quickly. I prayed.

Kenya is still a priority on my bucket list. It is time to head back to my "other" home!

KENYA

"Whenever a culture makes no sense to us, we must assume that the problem is ours, because the people's behavior makes sense to them"

(Paul G. Hiebert)

4

LEARNING THROUGH CHANGE

Changes

After a four year absence from Kenya, I finally returned "home." I was even happy to be on the brutally long journey of four different airplanes and thirty hours of travel! I was heading back to Kenya! This trip though, would be much different from the previous six trips. I would not be teaching at the seminary, but I would be investigating allegations and rumors that I knew were untrue concerning Nathan, and reconnecting with my Kenyan friends. Mostly I went to show support to Nathan and his family, and attempt to understand how cultural differences can cloud judgments and get in the way of genuine Christian love. When we do not seek to understand others, we often hurt them. I wanted to learn how to avoid and heal such pain.

I know life never stays the same and that many things can change in four years, but I was surprised at the extent of the changes I saw this year in Kenya. One positive change was something I viewed as progress; instead of driving for seven or eight hours from Nairobi to Kitale, there was now a small airport in Kitale, and I could take a one-hour flight from the Nairobi airport, to my "home" in Kitale. Unfortunately, I had a 6:00 am flight–the only flight of the day to Kitale, so I had to leave the guest house in Nairobi at 4:30 am. I was excited to see Nathan and to be back in Kitale, so the early flight did not bother me at all.

I boarded a small plane and soon arrived "home." Stepping out of the plane, I walked onto the small runway to the tiny one- room airport, and I immediately saw Nathan standing outside waiting to welcome me with a huge smile. We both laughed and greeted each other for a long time...so happy to re-connect. Nathan looked the same, though I knew he had gone through some trials and difficulties that I was yet to discover completely. Nathan grabbed my luggage, threw it in his car, and off we went.

The first thing Nathan did was take me to breakfast, assuming I had not eaten since I had such an early start to my day. Nathan was always so considerate. As we ate, we began to share what each of us had done and gone through since we last were together. Other than his family, Nathan was basically alone. In my past visits, Nathan's house was always filled with Americans; donors, supporters, friends, and people who loved him and wanted to be a part of whatever he was doing. I also was one of them, though I appeared to be the only one left. Many of Nathan's friends and supporters had abandoned him. Though four years had passed and so much had changed, I felt like I had just left Kitale and we were picking up from where we left off. In my heart, and in what I was observing, I knew that was not the case.

Changes from American "Friends"

Nathan told me how the American missionaries in Kitale, who were once close friends, no longer, spoke to him; if they saw him on the street, they would cross over or put their heads down and pretend they did not see him. Nathan said he has intentionally approached his former missionary friends, stood directly in front of them to speak, and to tell them he still loves them. Unfortunately, Nathan's former friends simply say, "I'm sorry Nathan," and walk away. Nathan said this break of friendships has hurt him deeply, and he did not fully understand what happened. I continued to eat, and to listen, but I did not fully understand it myself either.

All of Nathan's American financial support had ceased, and, being a Third World country, Nathan knew the Kenyans still needed some financial assistance. The Americans, who had formerly been the primary supporters of Nathan in America, said that Nathan's SELIDEF ministry should have been self-sustaining within five years, without the need for financial assistance from America; since the ministry was not self-sustaining, they stopped financial support and broke ties with him. Nathan had relayed that information to me previously (about the ending of his financial support), but he did not fully understand why. I was also confused; so, prior to my return to Kenya, I had called the supporters and asked one of the men why they stopped funding SELIDEF. He told me the same thing: Nathan was not self-sustaining.

I thought the idea of a Third World country becoming self-sustaining within five years was absurd, and I asked this supporter if he thought that was even feasible, to which he replied, "Probably not." Why then, would they continue to hold that point of view? I did not get a straight, honest, logical answer. Nathan could not at all understand this concept of Christians refusing to help one another after a certain time frame. I admit I could not understand that "logic" either.

Nathan also told me about a close friend from America who visited often each time he was in Kenya and who Nathan and his family loved dearly. I also knew this man, I will call Sam (not his real name), from the seminary where I taught. Sam was asked years ago to pray at the grounds of the first SELIDEF energy center, which was yet to be built, and to ask God's blessings upon this new ministry. Nathan said Sam was in tears at the thought of this ministry project, and was honored and humbled to be a part of its inception. Joshua and I had both met Sam on previous visits to Kenya and also liked him; we all became friends while together in Kenya. Nathan has not heard from Sam for years, even though he knows Sam has been in Kenya several times, without making contact. As we finished breakfast, I could see the pain and confusion on Nathan's face, but more so, I could sense the peace of God in his voice, and I knew that Nathan fully trusted God, whom he calls Papa, despite the pain and betrayal. Nathan said he still loves his American friends and has forgiven them, though his pain is deep.

Changes from Kenyan "Friends"

Nathan graciously paid for our breakfast and off we went through the streets of Kitale. Nathan knew I wanted to see my tree which was planted years ago at the SELIDEF headquarters in Kitale, so that was the first place he took me. My tree stood at the corner of the tree "lot" and now, it was the tallest tree there. Nathan took me over to it, and we hugged and laughed and took turns posing in front of it for our picture. I was so happy to see that my tree was so tall and healthy. My son's tree was a small pine that grew out, rather than up as mine did, and while healthy, we laughed at how short it was in comparison. We philosophized about the differences in the trees, enjoying our particular philosophies about life and ministry, and continued to laugh and to take pictures. I knew I was home.

We went into the SELIDEF building and Nathan shared more of his painful story that has unraveled over the last four years. Nathan's closest friend, I will call Pete (not his real name), was currently filing a lawsuit against Nathan, along with the former supporters and friends from America. Pete and these other supporters, claim that the SELIDEF ministry does not belong to Nathan, the money given and received does not belong to Nathan, and they want it all back for themselves, in an attempt to strip Nathan of everything. Despite careful and thorough audits, the lawsuit claims that Nathan has misappropriated funds. The audits prove otherwise. I could hardly believe that a lawsuit had been filed, but Nathan showed me the huge volumes of paperwork, and the court trial was set. I immediately thought of the Scripture in I Corinthians where Paul wrote about the sin of Christians suing one another:

"I challenge any of you who has a complaint against another to go to law before the unjust, and not before the saints. Do you not know that it is the saints who shall judge the world? And if the world will be judged by you, are you unworthy to judge the smallest matters? Do you not know that we shall even judge angels? How much more things that pertain to everyday life? If you have matters to be judged about this life, set them before the least esteemed in the assembly. I speak to arouse your sense of shame. Can you not find one man with enough sense to judge between his brethren? Yet brother goes to law against brother and that before unbelievers. Going to law with each other is evidence that your faith is not working. Why not rather be wronged? Why not rather be deprived? But you do wrong and cheat your brethren" (I Corinthians 6:1-8 DNT).

By this Scripture above, I can attest to the side following Christ. Pete is the same man who years ago sent me that painful email stating that I was not welcome to stay long-term in Kenya, without any explanation. I was now thankful that I did not come, and I felt God's protection from a painful and messy situation. Nathan's Kenyan "brothers" in the Lord have been trying for years to catch him in some wrongful act, but have been unsuccessful. Nathan is, and continues to be a man of God.

As Nathan and I walked around the SELIDEF compound, we approached a far corner where some bricks from the compound fence had obviously been replaced. Underneath these new bricks was a small opening where water flowed out from the compound, which now had small iron bars to fill in the gap. A couple of years ago, the SELIDEF office had been broken into in this area. Several thieves came during the night and dug out these bricks, then crawled through the small opening, which at the time did not have the bars welded in place. They ransacked the offices and stole all of the computers, hoping to find evidence against Nathan; they failed. While there were security guards at the compound, they did not have guns (which they have now), and they were tied up while this crime took place. Fortunately, no one was hurt, even though the thieves were heavily armed. Nathan found this terrible scene the following morning and immediately went to the police. However, the police actually told Nathan that this case would probably not be investigated, and no one was ever caught for this crime; it basically went unnoticed. Nathan was able to eventually get new computers and kept SELIDEF ministries going, though finances forced him to lay off most of his staff except for a few loyal employees. Nathan said his Kenyan "friends" keep trying to catch him doing something wrong, but they continue to fail. This lawsuit seems to be a final attempt.

Blessings in Disguise

Nathan had been receiving old, corroded batteries to sell to the rural Kenyans, who lived in the SELIDEF areas. Of course, they did not work, and Nathan was quite embarrassed; he had to refund their money and figure out what to do next. Nathan of course, did not know the batteries were used when he received them since they were tightly wrapped, clean, and looked new. When this problem of the defective batteries became apparent, Nathan had an engineer friend look into the matter. Nathan was not only embarrassed, but he was also upset that he was given defective products to sell which caused him to look bad, and which began the decline of the SELIDEF ministry.

Through a series of events and people that God placed in Nathan's life, Nathan discovered an even better source of light: solar lamps. There was no longer the need to have the batteries recharged each month. There was no longer the issue of how to dispose of old batteries. There was no longer the worry of being sold defective batteries. The solar lamps were a much better product, with far less problems, and were easier to use. Scripture records, which I believe applies in this situation that what man meant for evil, God used for good. In Genesis 50:20, it is recorded, *"As for you, you meant evil against me, but God meant it for good, to bring it about that many people should be kept alive, as they are today."*

Interesting Lodging

My conversations with Nathan and my learning would continue; but, for now, I needed to get checked into the guest house where I would be staying for my time here in Kitale. Nathan took me to my new home, the guest house, and before I was even checked in, we were bombarded with Canadian guests who wanted to know who we were and what we were doing here! Both Nathan and I were shocked with the boldness of these people, but we both tried to be polite and introduced ourselves. One of the men who descended upon us was from Canada, and was here with his wife, who quickly came to join in on the introductions. The Canadian couple came to do organic gardening, and to make Kenya, "The healthiest country in the world." However, in their attempt to obtain this lofty ambition, they needed to change the centuries-old Kenyan way of eating, which Nathan and I knew would not happen. This Canadian couple asked us to see their project and to show us their garden, but Nathan politely told them that I was not even checked into my room yet, and he wanted to make sure I was settled and unpacked before checking into other people's ministry projects. Feeling uncomfortable with my new fellow travelers, I was grateful for Nathan's diplomacy.

The groundskeeper took Nathan and me to my room, which was clean and simple. There was a kitchen, a small table with two chairs, a bathroom and two bedrooms. I would be sharing this home with another missionary woman from Canada, who was gone for the weekend but who would return Monday. I was not excited about sharing the house with a stranger, but I had done that before at other missionary guest houses, and it only cost me $10 per night, so I was grateful. The house was much nicer than I expected for the price, and with much gratitude, I thanked Nathan for booking this room for me. At least I would have a couple of days to myself to settle in before my roommate came home.

Cultural Clashes

The people who descended upon Nathan and me upon arrival returned once again to tell me about their ministry. Upon their past visits to Kenya, my Canadian "friends" found the Kenyan diet to be quite unhealthy (which it is), and they were determined to change it! The Kenyan diet has a lot of starch, including a great deal of corn, white rice, and the staple food *ugali*, which is maize (corn) flour and water, and is eaten every day. Kenyans love *ugali*, and it is cheap and filling. Kenyans believe *ugali* gives them strength and energy for the entire day, and they would never even consider going one day without eating it. Kenyans will never stop eating *ugali*; it is a large part of their culture. However, these Canadian missionaries started an organic farm, and they wanted to teach Kenyans how to change their diets to more greens, which Kenyans eat, though they fry them. The Canadian missionaries prohibited frying, and they wanted Kenyans to eat the greens raw. These Canadian missionaries also wanted to reduce the starch in the Kenyan diet, including the removal of *ugali*.

As an American who is a vegetarian and rather health conscious and particular about my diet, I thought this was a good idea, but not for Kenyans. Americans and Canadians cannot come into another culture and radically change their way of life, which they enjoy, because we think it is unhealthy. I began to understand the mistake of so many missionaries through this simple example of food. Many missionaries' hearts are in the right place, and like these organic farmers, they want what is good for others, though the means in accomplishing this good often appears arrogant and simply does not work. Kenyans will not remove ugali from their diet, no matter what an organic farmer tells them.

My roommate came home Monday, with the same ideas as her fellow Canadians about the need to change the Kenyan culture. She was a kind woman who was friends with these organic farmers, and she was more than welcoming to me, even though I was invading her space where she has lived for the past three years. However, she was more than happy to allow another woman to rent out the second bedroom and she said she welcomed the company. My roommate also spoke of the need to change the Kenyan's diet, and she hoped to change other aspects of their culture. For example, Canadians and Americans are punctual and time conscious; Kenyans, similar to much of the world, are not. She insisted on changing their way of thinking about time and becoming more punctual.

How arrogant we often are (though perhaps unaware), in thinking our way of life is superior to another culture, and, in the name of Christ, we come in as outsiders in an attempt to change people who are perfectly content with some of their ways. Unless a culture is living in sin, contrary to the Bible, or desperate for change themselves, perhaps we need to learn to leave well enough alone and to ask for wisdom in what to change and what to leave alone; this task can be quite challenging.

One example concerning time comes from the Arab culture. In parts of Arabia, if people agree on meeting at 9:00, only the servant shows up at 9:00, in obedience to his master. What is considered the "proper time" to arrive is actually between 9:45 and 10:15, which is the time expected. An American would think that the Arab has no sense of time and is inconsiderate, while the Arab would think the American is acting like a servant, and the Arab would therefore lose respect for the American. "Whenever a culture makes no sense to us, we must assume that the problem is ours, because the people's behavior makes sense to them" (Hiebert, 1976, p. 378).

My roommate also spoke about the need to change the Kenyan schools, since she said they are deficient in comparison to Canadian and American schools. When I asked her in what manner the schools are deficient, she said the students do not debate or ask enough questions, but rather just listen and take notes without question. Having lived in Chicago all of my life, and then moving to rural Kentucky, I immediately thought about the vast difference in those two cultures, and I compared that difference to the Kenyan vs. Canadian or American school systems. Chicagoans, in general, are more confrontational and direct than rural Kentuckians. A student in Appalachia would probably not debate or ask as many questions as a student in Chicago, simply because of the culture in which he/she lives, and what that culture deems polite and appropriate. Similar cultural difference occurs in Kenya, which is a culture of subtleties and politeness of which is closer to the Kentucky culture than the Chicago culture. Different teaching and learning styles will naturally exist within different cultural settings; one is not necessarily superior or inferior to another, but is dependent upon the culture from which it stems.

I asked my roommate how so many Kenyans/Africans can come to America, Canada or Europe for advanced studies, and earn Masters and Doctoral degrees, unless they have been properly educated before they came? I have several friends who have done well in American Universities, who are more educated than my roommate and me; yet, they came through the Kenyan school system. Perhaps the Kenyan school system is not deficient, but merely culturally different from what some of us may know. How arrogance can so subtlety creep into our minds, often in the name of Christ, without ourselves even being aware. I need to keep a check on myself as well.

An Indigenous Perspective

I spoke to Nathan about the conversations I had with my new Canadian acquaintances, pertaining to the cultural changes they as "missionaries" felt the need to make. I wanted to get a Kenyan perspective on outsiders, namely missionaries, who try to change Kenyan culture, "for their own good." Nathan shook his head and laughed, and told me that he finds that attitude quite arrogant. Nathan, along with other Kenyan friends of mine, said that when people from another country come into a foreign land and try to impose their values and their ideas of good, the indigenous culture views that attitude of needed change as one of superiority, and in the name of Jesus, an attitude that says, "We are smarter and know better than you." I quickly learned that while my Kenyan friends were polite and appeared interested in what these Canadians were doing and in what they thought, they were merely showing Christian love, beneath feelings of insult and offence.

Another problem that missionaries often have is that they do not ask the people who they are serving what they need and how they can help, which the indigenous people find degrading and insulting. To come into an area that is different from your own culture, and to tell people what you want to do for them for their benefit is rather arrogant. Perhaps the people you want to serve do not have any desire for the changes you as a missionary want to make, like taking ugali out of the Kenyan diet! I have yet to meet a Kenyan who finds the eradication of ugali a desirable change, and, as far as I can read in Scripture, ugali will not prohibit entrance into the Kingdom of God. Missionaries need to respect the culture in which they become a part of and ask the people they came to serve what they want, rather than tell them what they need.

At dinner one night, Nathan told me that another common mind-set of many missionaries is that a Kenyan cannot do anything on their own, or discover their own ways of ministry; instead, they need the help, guidance, and intelligence of a European or American. This mindset is an extremely arrogant and elitist way of thinking that still prevails in many parts of the world. Nathan said he has often been made to feel like he can do nothing without an outsider's help. However, if there is any sense that Nathan is getting ahead and growing in power, or even acquiring more than an American, then the Americans often pull out and leave him on his own. Nathan said Kenyans complain that American missionaries often make them feel like they need to beg and be subservient to their help, and if a Kenyan appears stronger or wealthier than an American, the American is not happy and will abandon the Kenyan; Nathan believes that is what happened with him and with SELIDEF.

Culture Shock

Nathan and a woman from the SELIDEF office took me on a life-changing trip that helped me understand what a missionary can do to help a culture, without offending and insulting. Nathan picked us up in a large four wheel drive truck, which he said we would need for this adventure. We drove out of Kitale, through several towns, and into a beautiful remote, mountainous area that was breathtaking. Lush green hills, forests, grass and mountains surrounded us as we began the ascent up the gravel mountain roads. I asked Nathan to stop along the way so I could take some pictures, in my attempt to capture and remember this Kenyan scenery. We were headed into the East Pokot tribal area; a primitive nomadic Kenyan tribe, whose wealth consisted of their cattle. The Pokot way of life, remember, was to engage in cattle raids, which involved sneaking into another family's area, killing the people and stealing their cattle. Their diet consisted mainly of cow's milk, cow's blood, and, on occasion, their meat.

I asked Nathan to stop the truck at a particular site that overlooked forests and hills, as we were in fairly high elevation by this time. The three of us got out to look out over God's creation, as we climbed a rocky hill and I took some pictures. Out of nowhere, a Pokot woman came running over to me yelling, *"Muzungu"* and grabbed me to hug me. She looked like a nomadic shepherd woman, barefoot, and dirty. I was pleasantly delighted to see her and returned her hugs, though trying not to show my offense at her odor; I wondered how long it had been since she bathed. I felt ashamed for even thinking about her odor, but it was rather strong. She spoke quickly to me in a language I could not understand, and she smiled, hugged, and touched me. I wondered if she had ever seen a *muzungu* (white person) before. A couple of small, dirty, barefoot children suddenly appeared from behind the rocks as well, and they too wanted to have a closer look at me, though they appeared frightened. I assumed these children belonged to this woman. They kept their distance.

These rural, nomadic Pokot people truly live different lives than I had ever seen. Most of their homes were mud huts with thatched roofs, built in this cool, rainy, desolate area of Kenya. I could not begin to imagine how their lives must be.

Back in the truck, we continued on and finally reached our destination: the East Pokot SELIDEF center. As always, Nathan had people there to meet and greet me, and to welcome me to this place. As usual, I was humbled. A large group of small, screaming, laughing children ran up to see me, as they too had probably never seen a *muzungu*! They wanted to hear me speak, and they wanted to touch my hair and skin in their wonderment. I laughed with the children and hugged them as we spoke the universal language of love through our touch, through our smiles, and through mere presence.

Cultural Lessons

After seeing the SELIDEF center and hearing about how these Pokot people are beginning to use their solar lamps and cooking stoves, I was taken to another building that taught me the wisdom of mission work: look for a way to improve an already existing way of life, but remove the sin, and bring ideas for abundance and happiness for the glory of God, without arrogance or offense. I also realized the value of having a vision, of looking at a violent culture, removing the sin, while retaining the culture.

If a Pokot becomes a Christian, and the cattle raids are a way of life, how then can that Christian live? Years ago I had asked that same question to Jackson. The answer now seemed obvious: build a dairy! If the wealth of these people lies in their cattle, instead of killing people to take their cattle, why not milk the cows, start a dairy, and sell the milk for profit? The Pokot culture at this SELIDEF area changed by ending the sin of violence, while the cattle remained the focal point of their lives and their economy; so now, within this Pokot culture, one could also live as a Christian.

The beauty of this dairy is that it improved lives forever, it gave people hope, it gave them something to wake up to and do, it employed many workers, and it gave people purpose. The cows were milked, and the milk was placed in plastic jugs that were loaded onto donkeys, which carried the milk to the dairy. In the more remote areas, a large tractor went to collect the milk into jugs and drove back to the dairy where the milk was pasteurized, cooled, and driven to Nairobi once a week to sell at the stores. Because the Pokot's wealth was their cattle, these people would also try to acquire as many cattle as possible, which meant they could not possibly use all of the milk that was available. The dairy then also prevented waste, and all of the milk could be used, both for themselves and for sale.

The Pokot in this area seemed to be most pleased with this new and meaningful way of life, which also caused them to think about why people would spend so much time and energy in their remote village, which in turn led them to the Gospel of Jesus Christ. Visions of solar lights, cooking stoves and a dairy completely and forever changed a violent and meaningless way of life, to a proud, productive and Christian way of life through the love and work of a few; this, is the work of missions. We now saw hope and purpose in the lives of many people in this rural, pastoral area; *"Hope encourages reason and gives it the strength to direct the will"* (Pope Benedict XVI, 2009, p.67).

This trip to the Pokot area of Kenya was the most meaningful and important part of my Kenyan experience this year, in addition to the fun and enjoyment of this most memorable day. More than any other event, conversation, seminar or training, this day taught me what mission work really is and how to work with a culture rather than to try to fight against it. Kenyan Christian leaders can show American missionaries how to transform individual lives, as well as entire communities, without arrogance or offense. I learned how to work within a culture and transform that culture to bring Jesus to them, rather than try to completely change a culture in the name of Jesus. Uneducated, untrained Kenyans taught me more this day than any graduate professor ever could. Coming to East Pokot transformed my life and my way of thinking about mission work; thank you Nathan for taking a day to bring me there.

Goliaths

The way of life in this Pokot area is rather harsh and difficult, partly because of the mountain terrain and the isolation of this rural area, and partly because of their primitive, nomadic way of life. Nathan's life has also has had many challenges and hardships in these past few years, yet he always expresses thanks and gratitude for these difficulties. On our long drive back to Kitale, Nathan spoke of his challenges as his "Goliath." I asked him what he meant, after he repeated "Goliath" about ten times. Kenyans pronounce Goliath so much differently than Americans that I had absolutely no idea what he was saying. I asked Nathan if he was using a Swahili or an English word when he said, "Goliath," since I could not understand him. I finally figured out what Nathan was saying when he said, "You know, the big man who David killed!" We laughed until we cried, and I quickly discovered that communication between various cultures can be difficult simply by the accents and the way particular words are pronounced, which can cause great misunderstandings.

Nathan referred to the story of David and Goliath as found in I Samuel 17, and he said that without Goliath, no one would have known who David was or the nature of his courage and faith in God. If there was no Goliath, David would not have stepped out and killed him with his sling and proven his faith in a God whom he knew would prevail.

Scripture records David telling Goliath, to his face,

"You come to me with a sword and with a spear and with a javelin, but I come to you in the name of the Lord of hosts, the God of the armies of Israel whom you have defied. This day the Lord will deliver you into my hand, and I will strike you down and cut off your head. And I will give the dead bodies of the host of the Philistines this day to the birds of the air and to the wild beasts of the earth that all the earth may know that there is a God in Israel, and that all the assembly may know

that the Lord saves not with sword and spear. For the battle is the Lord's." (I Samuel 17:45-47a).

Nathan and I spoke about this idea of "Goliaths" in the context of SELIDEF and in the betrayal of so many of his friends. Without this "Goliath" in his life right now, others could not see how powerful and loving God is to those who love Him and desire to serve Him with their whole heart. Nathan spoke of the power of God shining forth through our "Goliaths," which was also true in the Exodus. Nathan gets excited when he anticipates what God is going to do for those who trust Him, and how God works completely contrary to the way the world works, as He did with David and Goliath.

I also thought of how our "Goliaths" prove to others that we believe in a mighty and powerful God, full of love and compassion beyond our wildest imaginations. Without his "Goliath," others could not see Nathan's unwavering faith in a God whom he knows will sustain him and remain faithful to him, even when all of his friends are gone. Without his "Goliath," others could not see Nathan's ability to love and to forgive those who have betrayed and hurt him, which Nathan can only do because of the Holy Spirit who lives in him and enables him. The battle, like David said, is truly the Lord's.

For those of us who love God with all of our heart, our mind, our body and our soul, and who come willingly into full submission to Him, God will indeed bring about "Goliaths." It is in our attitudes and how we handle these "Goliaths," that God uses us, or does not use us and finds another "David." I do not want to lose heart, to fear, or to lack faith, and therefore miss out on a wonderful plan God has for my life and in ways He wants to use me. May I learn to welcome the "Goliaths" in my life, pass the tests, and watch God work in ways I would have never imagined. May I run towards my Goliath as David did, and become all that God intended for me to be.

The Shunammite Woman

I spent the following morning alone, reflecting on my trip so far, on cultural blunders, on lost friendships, on decreased funding, on "Goliaths," and on broken dreams. I was reminded of a teaching I heard years ago from Phil Vischer, the founder of the famous Christian cartoon, "Veggie Tales." He gave a lesson from 2 Kings 4:8-37, about the Shunammite woman and Elisha. Here is the story:

"One day Elisha went to Shunem. And a well-to-do woman was there, who urged him to stay for a meal. So whenever he came by, he stopped there to eat. She said to her husband, 'I know that this man who often comes our way is a holy man of God. Let's make a small room on the roof and put in it a bed and a table, a chair and a lamp for him. Then he can stay there whenever he comes to us.'

One day when Elisha came, he went up to his room and lay down there. He said to his servant Gehazi, 'Call the Shunammite.' So he called her, and she stood before him. Elisha said to him, 'Tell her, you have gone to all this trouble for us. Now what can be done for you? Can we speak on your behalf to the king or the commander of the army?' She replied, 'I have a home among my own people.' 'What can be done for her?' Elisha asked. Gehazi said, 'She has no son, and her husband is old.' Then Elisha said, 'Call her.' So he called her, and she stood in the doorway. 'About this time next year,' Elisha said, 'you will hold a son in your arms.' 'No, my lord!' she objected. 'Please, man of God, don't mislead your servant!' But the woman became pregnant, and the next year about that same time she gave birth to a son, just as Elisha had told her.

The child grew, and one day he went out to his father, who was with the reapers. He said to his father, 'My head! My head!' His father told a servant, 'Carry him to his mother.' After the servant had lifted him up and carried him to his mother, the boy sat on her lap until noon, and then he died. She went up and laid him on the bed of the man of God, then shut the door and went out. She called her husband and said, 'Please send me one of the servants and a donkey so I can go to the man of God quickly and return.' 'Why go to him today?'

he asked. 'It's not the New Moon or the Sabbath.' 'That's all right,' she said. She saddled the donkey and said to her servant, 'Lead on; don't slow down for me unless I tell you.' So she set out and came to the man of God at Mount Carmel.

When he saw her in the distance, the man of God said to his servant Gehazi, 'Look, there's the Shunammite! Run to meet her and ask her, are you all right? Is your husband all right? Is your child all right?' 'Everything is all right," she said. When she reached the man of God at the mountain, she took hold of his feet. Gehazi came over to push her away, but the man of God said, 'Leave her alone! She is in bitter distress, but the Lord has hidden it from me and has not told me why.' 'Did I ask you for a son, my lord?' she said. 'Didn't I tell you, don't raise my hopes?' Elisha said to Gehazi, 'Tuck your cloak into your belt, take my staff in your hand and run. Don't greet anyone you meet, and if anyone greets you, do not answer. Lay my staff on the boy's face.' But the child's mother said, 'As surely as the Lord lives and as you live, I will not leave you.' So he got up and followed her. Gehazi went on ahead and laid the staff on the boy's face, but there was no sound or response. So Gehazi went back to meet Elisha and told him, 'The boy has not awakened.'

When Elisha reached the house, there was the boy lying dead on his couch. He went in, shut the door on the two of them and prayed to the Lord. Then he got on the bed and lay on the boy, mouth to mouth, eyes to eyes, hands to hands. As he stretched himself out on him, the boy's body grew warm. Elisha turned away and walked back and forth in the room and then got on the bed and stretched out on him once more. The boy sneezed seven times and opened his eyes. Elisha summoned Gehazi and said, 'Call the Shunammite.' And he did. When she came, he said, 'Take your son.' She came in, fell at his feet and bowed to the ground."

What Vischer taught through this Scripture in 2 Kings, is that we often have dreams, big dreams, concerning our ministries, our work, or our missionary responsibilities, which are good, but they can be taken away or transformed in ways we did not anticipate.

In this story in 2 Kings, the Shunammite woman was childless, and was married to an older man who would more than likely die before her. In the culture in which she lived, when her husband died, this Shunammite woman would have no means of support, since the children took care of their parents. A Kenyan person would understand this concept, since in their culture the oldest son is responsible to care for the parent left alone. The Shunammite woman had a real need, that appeared would go unmet. Elisha came into her life and promised a solution to her problem, and he informed her that she would indeed have a child.

The Shunammite woman begged Elisha not to tease her with such hope, because she was certain it would not transpire, and a dashed hope can hurt more than no hope at all. However, the following year, just as Elisha prophesied, this woman did indeed have a son, who as we can imagine, brought her not only great joy and love as most mothers have for their children, but financial security when her husband would die; then, the unthinkable happens: her son died! Phil Vischer compares the death of this boy to the death of some of our greatest hopes and dreams. I thought of my broken dream of moving to Kenya several years ago to teach full time at the seminary...

Nathan, his wife, and his staff at SELIDEF had great dreams of SELIDEF and of an ever-expanding ministry that would reach many people in Africa. Just as the Shunammite woman's son died, it appeared that Nathan's ministry too might die, since his funding had stopped and his friends abandoned him. The pain of realized dreams that are later broken, are probably more painful than never having a dream attained. One cannot wonder why God would allow great joy and satisfaction only to strip it away. As I spoke about this biblical lesson with Nathan, I told him that I was confident that, like the Shunammite woman's son, SELIDEF would also be resurrected and would be more powerful than when it began. Nathan, with his usual strong and unwavering faith, smiled and agreed.

Cultural Lessons to Take Back Home

On Sunday, Nathan and his family took me to their home church in Kitale, which resembled an American church. The service lasted about an hour, with worship, sharing, prayer, an offering, and the sermon. However, Nathan wanted me to have a unique worship experience, so we then all went to another church, which was another one of the highlights of my Kenyan trip this year.

We drove into a small, rural area, to a church made out of mud, surrounded by mud huts where the people from this congregation live. This particular church had never had an American visitor, and many of the people in this small congregation had never seen a white person! Little did I realize that Nathan went through a great deal of preparation prior to visiting this church, just for me! Nathan wanted me to attend a church unlike any I had ever been in before, but he also wanted to ensure that the pastor's theology was biblically correct, and the teaching was centered on Christ. To ensure the truth of the church's focus, Nathan actually called and interviewed several pastors in rural areas, and spoke to the pastor of this church who gave solid biblical answers that satisfied Nathan. He also wanted to make sure this church never had an American visitor, which the pastor conceded they had not. Upon deciding on this particular congregation, Nathan called the pastor the Friday before we arrived, to confirm that we would be joining them for worship. How many Americans do you know would go through all of that trouble to take a visitor to church?

Upon our arrival at the small mud church, Nathan, his wife, their daughter, and me, were asked to sit up front, in four chairs alongside the pulpit, for the four of us guests, while the congregation sat on benches, with the women on one side, and the men on the other. While all Kenyans who have been to school speak English, many Kenyans in these rural areas only speak Swahili and their own tribal dialect since they have not had the opportunity for formal education. Knowing this fact, I assumed that this worship service would be spoken in Swahili, and if I was fortunate, there might be someone to translate so I would understand the message and all that would be spoken. To my amazement, the pastor said in honor of their first American visitor, the service would be spoken entirely in English, and translated into Swahili for his congregation! I was truly amazed.

As is the usual custom in Kenyan churches, I was asked to speak and to bring greetings from America. However, because of the amazing hospitality from the people of this church, I was speechless. I went up front as asked, and I told those brothers and sisters in Christ that I could not really think of anything to say, and that I felt overwhelmed by their kindness. Their hospitality and their warmth far surpassed any church I had ever visited in America. I have moved many times and I have visited many different churches, and often no one even spoke to me. Never had I experienced anything quite like what I had experienced in this humble mud church building.

While I was speaking about their kindness, a woman was asked to come up by me, and what she did next almost knocked me to my knees; the church had bought me a gift that she presented to me! She had a beautiful piece of cloth that many Kenyan women use to wrap around themselves like a dress or a shawl. I could not believe it! This woman from this poor church gently wrapped the cloth around my body, tied a knot near my shoulder, and gave me a huge hug. I was literally brought to tears. I spoke briefly about how I felt and how they modeled Jesus to me. I, a total stranger, now felt like family. I asked everyone to stand and hold hands, and I prayed for this church, for each person in it, and, of course, for my dear friend Nathan and his family, for going through the work of finding this church and bringing me here.

After the worship service (which, according to a sign on the church wall, went from 5:00 a.m. to 1:00 p.m. each

Sunday), the pastor asked us to go next door to the church office to visit with one another. The pastor and the leaders of the church accompanied Nathan, his wife, their daughter, and me to the office, which was small mud hut, and water and sodas were brought for all of us to drink. Fruit was also brought in, but only for us visitors to eat, and we talked and shared, and quickly became friends and family.

I loved this little mud church, and I told the pastor and the church leaders in this hut that if I ever moved to Kenya, this church would be my home church; this simple statement brought smiles and great joy to these most loving people. What a beautiful Sunday I experienced here in rural Kenya, thanks to the love of my Kenyan family and friends. What a delightful culture shock I encountered! I was truly blessed, and I learned a great lesson from my new friends in Christ. Mission work is always reciprocal.

With my good friend Nathan to help me, and to speak openly and honestly about cultural ideas, needs and desires, I wanted to get on board and get my little rural church in Kentucky involved in Kenya and with mission work. A "Goliath" stood in front of me, but I was up to the challenge, since I believed, as David did, that the battle belongs to the Lord. The biggest, most powerful "Goliath" appeared to be the challenge of culture, where there was still so much for us all to learn.

Lord, let the Church and the people slay the Goliaths that hinder the advance of Christianity in foreign lands!

~

"I learned how to work within a culture and transform that culture to bring Jesus to them, rather than try to completely change a culture in the name of Jesus."

5

CONFRONTING CULTURAL DIFFERENCES

Defining Culture

Before talking about how to work cross-culturally and how to slay the "Goliaths" and confront cultural differences, we need first to define culture, cultural sensitivity and cultural understanding. Culture is defined in different ways, by many different people, and culture is more complicated than one normally thinks.

Anthropologist William Haviland defined culture as: *"A set of rules or standards shared by members of a society, which when acted upon by the members, produce behavior that feels within a range of variation the members consider proper and acceptable."* Haviland goes on to say that culture also includes, *"Abstract values, beliefs and perceptions of the world that lie behind people's behavior but which are reflected in their behavior. These are shared by members of a society, and when acted upon, they produce behavior considered acceptable within that society. Cultures are learned, largely through the medium of language, rather than inherited biologically, and the parts of a culture function as an integrated whole"* (*Cultural Anthropology*, Haviland, 1993, p.29).

Culture is therefore not necessarily observable behavior, but rather beliefs and values that people hold and use to, *"Interpret experience and generate behavior"* (Haviland, 1993, p.30).

Paul Hiebert, another anthropologist, defined culture as, *"The more or less integrated system of ideas, feelings and values, and their associated patterns of behavior and products shared by a group of people who organize and regulate what they think, feel and do"* (Hiebert, 1976, p. 30).

Yale Professor Lamin Sanneh defined culture as, *"An organic which is greater than the sum total of its parts, those parts being material, social and religious, with language as the system of symbolization for its explicit parts. Culture is transmissible and accumulative, and religious culture especially, depends on critical appropriation for its continuing integrity"* (Sanneh, 1989, p. 201). Sanneh also said, *"Essentially, culture is a human enterprise"* (Sanneh, p. 202).

Culture and Missions

So how should missionaries view culture, and live within cultures much different than their own, without disrespect and with sensitivity? An early Christian letter to Diognetus, written by an unknown author possibly in the second century, described the followers of Christ in this manner:

"For Christians cannot be distinguished from the rest of the human race by country or language or customs. They do not live in cities of their own; they do not use a peculiar form of speech; they do not follow an eccentric manner of life...yet, although they live in Greek and barbarian cities alike, as each man's lot has been cast, and follow the customs of the country in clothing and food and other matters of daily living, at the same time they give proof of the remarkable and admittedly extraordinary constitution of their own commonwealth.

They live in their own countries, but as aliens. They have a share in everything as citizens, and endure everything as foreigners. Every foreign land is their fatherland, and yet for them every fatherland is a foreign land. They marry and have children just like everyone else; but they do not kill their unwanted babies. They offer a shared table, but not a shared bed. They are at present in the flesh but they do not live 'according to the flesh.' They are passing their days on earth, but are citizens of heaven. They obey the appointed laws, and go beyond the laws of their own lives. They love everyone, but are persecuted by all. They are unknown and condemned; they are put to death and gain life. They are poor and yet make many rich. They are short of everything and yet have plenty of all things. They are dishonored and yet gain glory through dishonor. Their names are blackened and yet they are cleared. They are mocked and bless in return. They are treated outrageously and behave respectfully to others. When they do good, they are punished as evildoers; when punished, they rejoice as if being given new life. They are attacked by Jews as aliens, and are persecuted by Greeks; yet those who hate them cannot give any reason for their hostility. To put it simply–the soul is to the body as Christians are to the world. The soul is spread through all parts of the body and Christians through all the cities of the world. The soul is in the body but is not of the body; Christians are in the world but not of the world." {From (http://www.ccel.org/richardson/fathers.xi.ii.html) The Early Christian Fathers in, *"The So-called Letter to Diognetus"* by an anonymous writer}.

How does this quote above apply to mission work? Is Kenya a fatherland for me? Is America as alien to me as Kenya, since as a Christian, my real home is in Heaven? How does this concept of the Christian's role in the world, as written in this anonymous letter, relate to cultural sensitivity? Missionaries must first understand that Christians live in all parts of the world, in all types of cultures, and that the requirements of a Christ - follower have nothing to do with living as a westerner. If the need to bring in a "western" or "modern" way of life into a culture is done by missionaries, it can only be for pragmatic needs for reasons of health, environment, or quality of life, such as the changes implemented in Kenya with the cooking stoves, solar lamps, and the dairy. Also, whatever changes are introduced must be accepted and desired by the culture in which the changes are suggested, and never forced. Mission work has often been criticized as being, *"An unwarranted interference in other cultures"* (Sanneh, 1989, p.202). If missionaries interfere culturally in ways that are not desired, then their message of Jesus Christ will also be undesired.

East vs. West

There has been a great deal of controversy, mistakes, problems and disrespect within the Eastern and Western worlds of Christianity. For some reason, Christianity has been called a Western religion, and missionaries from the west have often felt the need to westernize people in the east when they brought the Gospel message. However, Christianity began in the Middle East. God chose Jesus to be born in Bethlehem, a town in the Middle East, where the Christian message was initially heard, and where the disciples also lived. The Bible was written primarily by Jewish people from the Middle East, and there is little western thought in Scripture. It was not until the apostle Paul took the Gospel to the Gentiles that any westerners even heard the message of Christianity.

So how is western thought defined, and how did the West come to be associated with Christianity? Western thought involves Greek philosophy/rationalism, Roman law, European languages, separation of Church and State, democratic representative governing bodies, individual rights and liberties, and Christianity. Islam, Hinduism and Buddhism are known as eastern religions (Huntington, 1996, p.70). When the Middle Eastern faith of Christianity was taken to the West, it more or less became known as the western religion, often intermingled and confused with democracy and western politics. According to political scientist Samuel Huntington, religion is one of the most important factors in defining culture, which is why Christianity came to be associated with western thought, while Islam came to be associated with eastern thought. Religion, according to Huntington, and not political or economic ideologies, is the biggest distinction among people of different cultures; this is the reason that Huntington believes there is a clash of cultures between the East and the West.

Western Culture/Modern Culture

Many missionaries from the West, who go to the East, often feel that, in order to bring the Good News of Jesus Christ, one must also bring western culture and modernize that culture as well. However, "modernize" and "westernize" are not synonymous. Western civilization emerged in the eighth and ninth centuries, but did not modernize until the seventeenth and eighteenth centuries (Huntington, 1996, p. 69). SELIDEF does indeed focus on modernizing the rural communities for various benefits, such as health, education, and environmental reasons, but it does not attempt to westernize the cultures. An American working with SELIDEF can perhaps "transform" the culture, while retaining the basic heart of the culture, but only if such transformations are desired by the indigenous culture.

Kenya is of course an eastern country, with eastern traditions and thoughts, but Kenya also has some western influence since it was colonized by the British. European and American missionaries have also tried to "westernize" Kenya, largely through arrogance and feelings of western superiority, much to the detriment of the Kenyans and the message of Jesus Christ in its pure, biblical form.

Christ and Culture

The ideas of the Christian message and the issue of human culture were addressed in a classic book written by Richard Nieburh, entitled, *Christ and Culture*. Nieburh wrote, *"Christ's answer to the problem of human culture is one thing. Christian answers are another"* (Nieburh, 1951, p. 2). According to Nieburh, culture was defined as, *"The total process of human activity"* which includes, *"language, habits, ideas, beliefs, customs, social organizations, inherited artifacts, technical processes and values"* (Nieburh, 1951, p. 32). Culture, according to Nieburh, is always social and is, *"The organization of human beings into permanent groups"* and always involves human achievement because it is, *"The work of men's minds and hands"* (Nieburh, 1951, p. 33). Nieburh believed that culture included, *"speech, education, tradition, myth, science, art, philosophy, government, law, rite, beliefs, inventions and technologies*" (Nieburh, 1951, p. 35), which are all based on values.

Culture therefore, defines values and is teleological; what we believe is good, is what we believe is good for us. Culture is concerned with what is good for men, women, children, adults, those who rule, and those who are ruled, according to the customary notions of such good (Nieburh, 1951, p. 38). There is therefore, an *"inherent tension"* (Nieburh, p. 34) between Christ and culture. Is there opposition between the teachings of Christ and various cultures, or is there agreement? If there is opposition, how do missionaries address this issue without resentment and disrespect for the culture in which they live and work? Here lies the "problem" of Christ and culture. Perhaps missionaries might be more understanding and effective if they tried to come to terms with this concept of Christ and culture. Richard Nieburh looked at five different possible relationships of Christ and culture, church and society.

Christ against Culture

The first position, which Nieburh called Christ *against* culture, involves people he calls "*separatists,*" who believe that Christ is against culture, so Christians must then separate themselves from the world. There needs to be a total separation or divorce so to speak, between Christ, Christians, the Church, and the world. Christ is the *wholly other* and is outside or in opposition to culture, *"For it is in culture that sin chiefly resides"* (Nieburh, 1951, p. 52). If sin is transmitted through culture, then missionaries view entering into a foreign culture as entering into sinful, enemy territory. People who hold this view believe that Christians should develop their own unique culture, entirely separate from any non-Christian society or culture.

If missionaries hold this view of Christ against culture, they might fall into the temptation of feeling superior, and feel a compulsion to disrespect and change a culture that is not Christian, even if certain aspects of that culture do not conflict with Scripture. People who hold this position notice that while Jesus sometimes challenged the Jewish culture of His day, He did not try to reform it, but simply ignored it, and He was therefore seen as a threat. The Scripture used to validate this position comes from 1 John 2:15 *"Love not the world, nor the things in the world. If anyone loves the world, the love of the Father is not in him."* (Green, DNT). Sin therefore arises not only out of our own sinful, human nature, but also out of culture itself.

The Christ of Culture

The second model that Nieburh presented is called the Christ *of* Culture, which is diametrically opposed to the first position. People who hold this view are called *"accomodationists,"* and see an almost total accommodation of Christ and Christianity to cultural expressions. Culture is seen in light of Christ, rather than in opposition to Him. Jesus was the fulfiller of culture and He can be interpreted *through* culture. In this model, Christians should build and establish community within the culture of unbelievers.

People who hold this view of the Christ of culture think the "separatists" are radical since they reject culture for the sake of Christ, and that any conflict between Christ and culture is due, *"To the church's misunderstanding of Christ"* (Nieburh, 1951, p. 91). Christians should be able to attain a peaceful cooperative in society, participating fully in culture, while still living out their Christian faith. When Christ is seen as the Christ of culture, then it is the task of Christians to maintain the best culture possible. Many different cultures are represented in the Bible, so the Gospel is, and needs to be, culturally universal.

This view of the Christ of culture has a danger of causing some people to identify Christianity with some socio-economic or political systems, and can make western missionaries feel culturally superior, since they might view their own culture as inherently Christian. A missionary might then feel the need to not only Christianize, but also to westernize a "heathen" culture who does not know Christ. Christianity has sometimes been identified with western democracy and capitalism, which is simply not accurate.

Christ above Culture

In this third model, people who hold this view of Christ *above* culture are called *"synthesists."* Christ neither arises nor contributes to culture, but instead, He enters into our human culture from above. The lordship of Christ is *above* culture, and there is no subordination of culture to faith. Sin is seen as moral and cultural imperfection, and cultural sin as social conflict is basically ignored. Both our faith and our redemption are seen as superior to culture, but do not contradict culture because they perfect culture. The fundamental issue here is not between Christ and culture, but between God and man. Jesus is Lord of both this world and the next.

Missionaries need to be in cooperation with non-Christians to work together, while maintaining a distinctive Christian life. There is probably less danger of cultural arrogance with people who hold this position as opposed to the previous models.

Christ and Culture in Paradox

The model of Christ and culture in paradox is similar to the model of Christ against culture, but it holds a more positive view of culture. People who hold this view are called *"dualists."* There is a polar tension in this model of "both" - "and," in that we need to, *"Distinguish between loyalty to Christ and responsibility to culture"* (Nieburh, 1951, p. 91). The conflict lies between God and man, and is not a matter of Christians vs. culture or the world; rather, there is a perpetual tension between culture and Christianity because of their different natures. Christians are called to obey Christ and to follow God rather than men, but Christians are also called to obey government and cultural institutions which, according to Scripture, are placed by God;

"Obey those who have rule over you, and line yourselves up under their authority: for they watch over your souls,

because they know they will have an account to give. Make it a grateful task for them: it is your loss if they find it a difficult task" (Hebrews 13:17 DNT).

Here lies the tension; Christ reveals human sin and is the judge and redeemer of culture. Christ and culture will have an unavoidable tension, since culture is corrupt and subject to judgment. The difference of this view with Christ against culture is that the emphasis is not on separation, but on dualism. The world is a sinful, Godless place, yet it is sustained by God, and it is in a struggle between promise and fulfillment.

Christ the Transformer of Culture

The final position of Nieburh's is labeled *Christ the transformer of culture*. People who hold this view are called *"conversionists."* This position is similar to the dualists, but it has an even more positive view of culture. God in Christ entered into human culture in order to transform it. Christians do not need to create a new culture, but merely transform or renew the sins that are found within the particular culture. The authority for this transformation is in Christ and in Scripture, which should be the only basis for transformation. Sin is seen as, *"A radical fall of human action and corruption,"* and culture as a, *"perverted good"* (Lecture in *Cross Cultural Ethics* at Northern Baptist Theological Seminary, Motessi, 2000). Any renewal in culture will not come directly through missionaries, but by God's grace and power, as He works *through* missionaries.

God's Kingdom can be established on earth by the work of Jesus Christ, and through the faithful discipleship of Christians and missionaries. There is a dialectical notion of history and society, and a Christocentric view of the relationship between Christ and culture. Culture is, *"The arena of God's mighty acts and of human response"* (Motessi, 2000). This view of Christ as the transformer of culture stems from the Gospel of John, when Jesus prayed to the Father and said,

"They are not of the world, even as I am not of the world. Make them holy through your truth: your word is truth. As you

delegated Me into the world, even so I have delegated them into the world" (John 17:16-18 DNT).

Differing Viewpoints

Because of these differing viewpoints which people hold in some form or another (though most people are probably unaware), there have been various approaches to mission work. Some of the arguments in Nieburh's book, *Christ and Culture,* concern Jesus' ignoring culture and teaching us to rely on God's grace alone, which atheists believe hinders full human potential. Christ and the early Church did not actually ignore culture but were intolerant towards aspects of culture, since, at that time, Christians violated some of the cultural norms found in the Roman society in which they lived and which were considered sacred, such as worship of the Emperor. Also, many of Christ's teachings are truly incompatible with society and culture, especially those teachings found in the Sermon on the Mount in the Gospel of Matthew, chapters 5-7, where Jesus gave examples of cultural practices, but taught us to transform those practices in accordance to His Word.

Ongoing debates continue among Christians in their attempt to reconcile Christ and culture, but Nieburh stressed throughout his book that the ultimate virtue of Christ is love, and that it must also be ours. Each of these five viewpoints of Christ and culture has a Scriptural basis or an interpretation of Scripture, and each model attempts to discern what Christ taught. Jesus did indeed challenge the culture of His day and He was indeed a threat to Jewish culture.

Judaism was more than a religion; it was a cultural way of life, yet Jesus refused to follow it when it strayed from Scripture, and He pointed out the hypocrisy and pride found in some of its teachings. In this respect, Jesus did indeed go against culture. Jesus also taught us to rely solely on God, yet He never wants to diminish our human potential. There were also times when Jesus was intolerant with the culture, such as when He turned over the tables in the Temple as recorded in

John 2:13-16. Jesus always went against culture when it was contrary to the laws of God. Jesus did indeed call us to be a peculiar people and to live separately from the world of culture, living in the world, but not of the world, which Jesus spoke about in his high priestly prayer as recorded in John 17.

Christianity is a radical way of life. We are called to live contrary to our sinful human nature, and to teach this truth to others in all cultures. The apostle Paul was able to masterfully move in and out of various cultures with great sensitivity in order to win people to Christ. Paul wrote,

"For though I am free from the authority of all men, yet have I made myself servant to all, that I might win more converts. And with the Jews I live as a Jew, that I might win Jews to Christ; to those under the law, I put myself under the law, that I might win them; to those without the law, as without law (being under the law of Christ), that I might win those that are without the law. To the weak, I become weak, that I might win the weak; I am made all things to all men that I might by all means save some. I am still doing this to advance the gospel, so that I may become a joint-partaker of the gospel with you" (1 Corinthians 9:19-23 DNT).

How then, does a missionary enter another culture with sensitivity, respect, love and truth? How does a missionary reconcile Christ and culture? The challenge might be much more difficult than one thinks.

Nieburh's models of Christ and culture do not need to be thought of individually, but they can be blended in various ways for effective mission work. Within the context of my work in Kenya and with SELIDEF, I lean towards the last model of Christ as the transformer of culture, especially in the context of the Pokot tribe and the dairy that was begun in that rural area. Missionaries have developed the Pokot's agricultural way of life and transformed it into the possibility of a Christian way of life through working with the milk from the cows for the good of the people, instead of living in a culture of violence through cattle raids and killings. The Pokot's culture can indeed be transformed through Christ. Nieburh's models have been used (probably unaware) throughout mission work, with some success, though also sometimes with failure.

Missions in History

Culture is something that is learned and transmitted from generation to generation, which is called "enculturation." Through enculturation, people learn the socially appropriate ways to satisfy basic human needs, such as food, shelter, companionship, self-defense and sexual gratification. Unless these human needs are contrary to Scripture, missionaries need to respect the cultural norms and learn to live within them in their respective culture; unfortunately, that has not always been the case.

From the beginning of the Christian faith, Jesus, a Jew, primarily taught other Jews; yet, He laid the groundwork for the Gentile mission using the apostle Paul (who was also Jewish). The emphasis on Paul's mission work was on teaching others about Jesus Christ and making disciples in whatever culture they lived. Mission work is about, *"Proclaiming the lordship of Christ, baptizing and teaching"* (Bosch, 1991, p. 78), which can be accomplished in many different ways.

The apostle Paul was the first person instructed to take the Gospel of Jesus Christ to another culture, the Gentiles, and he did so with cultural sensitivity and respect. We could say that Paul's mission was the first cross-cultural breakthrough, and he knew that God sees all cultures equally; *"God does not absolutize any one culture, whatever the esteem in which God holds culture"* (Sanneh, 1989, p. 47). God, through the work of dedicated, sensitive missionaries, can transform any non-Christian culture through the redeeming love of Christ.

Although Christianity started in the Middle East, it spread to the Western world, into the Roman Empire, and has been called a Western religion, while Islam is known as an Eastern religion. Christianity flourished in Western Europe and became rooted in the Greco-Roman culture. Unfortunately, western civilization and colonialism grew quite arrogant, and the white, western leaders of the Church believed their ways were the correct ways, and that they should have the last word on all subjects, including cultural practices and religious expression. Many western leaders believed that the western, colonial culture was superior to the rest of the world, which had little to contribute, and the Church absorbed these ideas; this self-centered mind-set began in the Roman Empire and in the Western Church, and was transplanted onto every other continent.

"The necessity of being like the Western Church in everything, except perhaps the color of the skin, was drilled with such intensity and urgency into the minds of its followers that it became a real pride for any church to claim that identity, sameness and uniformity" (Bellagama, 1992, p. 28).

Many western missionaries made their converts change to fit the western mold and to discard any local customs that clashed. The Western Church, both European and American, *"Allowed racial and religious pride to direct our attitude toward those whom we have been wont to call 'poor heathen'"* (Allen, 1997, p. 142), while acting as if they were superior and moved by charity, compassion and sympathy to help these poor souls. They apparently did not understand that they were simply instruments used by God, with the same Creator and Heavenly Father as the *"poor heathens"* whom they tried to save.

The colonialists (as well as some missionaries today), did not regard the people they were trying to reach as equals; *"We have done everything for them except give place to them, and treated them as 'dear children' and not as brethren"* (Allen, 1997, p. 143). Unfortunately, mission work has not always been done in the spirit of love and equality, and has sometimes failed to fulfill its role as Christ intended.

Criticisms of Mission Work

Some missionaries, especially those from the colonial West, have made huge blunders in bringing the Gospel to other parts of the world, especially on the continent of Africa. Cultural insensitivity and arrogance have probably been the biggest criticisms of mission work, and have caused the most damage. Some western missionaries criticized African worship, and considered it a, *"Weakness and a blemish that the new prophets encouraged with displays of extreme emotion and wild, raving shouts,"* relating this to an, *"Unredeemed African past"* (Sanneh, 1989, p. 153). T.J. Bowen, an American missionary once said, *"It is not enough to bring Africans the knowledge of Christ, they must be instructed in the arts of modernity"* (Sanneh, 1989, p. 164). Many missionaries, mostly from Britain, expected their African converts to also westernize in their clothing, *"To build square houses rather than round ones, to settle in a village around the church and school rather than in scattered homesteads; to change the division of labor between men and women, and to abandon ancient festivals, such as traditional dances, which were judged by the whites to be lewd"* (Sanneh, 1989, p. 175).

In the past, many missionaries criticized some African tribes for their loud worship styles, their drum beating, and their dancing, but there is certainly no one, correct way to worship God. For a tribe whose worship is loud, Scripture can justify that style, such as in Psalm 150:3-5

"Praise him with the sounding of the trumpet, praise him with the harp and lyre, praise him with the tambourine and dancing, praise him with the strings and flute, praise him with the clash of cymbals, praise him with resounding cymbals".

If a tribe worships quietly, Scripture can also justify that as well, as in Colossians 3:15-16 which says,

"And let the peace of God rule in your hearts, this will produce harmony and thankfulness to the church. Allow the word of Christ to remain in you as a treasure of wisdom, teaching and gently reminding one another in psalms and hymns and spiritual songs with grace in your hearts to the Lord " (DNT).

Unless there exists a style of worship which Scripture opposes, such as hurting or killing someone, missionaries need to respect and embrace the traditional cultural practices and worship styles. We cannot confuse the American style of worship (which is also diverse) with the Gospel. Missionaries today, "*Must safeguard the indigenous heritage*" (Sanneh, 1989, p. 112) of the people where they work, and cease pushing westernization and colonialism onto the east, including Africa, which has become the, "*Victim of Western cultural imperialism*" (Bellagamba, 1992, p. 46).

Economics has been another area of criticism within mission work. The word "economy" comes from the Greek word *oikonomia,* and refers to the management of one's household and stewardship. The basic concern of economics is in how people apply their, "*knowledge, skills and efforts to the gifts of nature in order to satisfy their material needs*" (Janda, 1996, p. 247).

Western missionaries have generally had more financial resources than the people in the East, especially in most African countries, of which their converts relied on the resources of their brothers and sisters in the West. However, over the years with political changes, tribal conflicts, interpersonal conflicts, or personal health and/or financial issues, many western missionaries have had to leave their African countries and return to the States, leaving the indigenous leaders on their own without the support they still needed.

In Kenya, Nathan and SELIDEF were left without the necessary funding and support to continue to thrive, since the American missionaries unrealistically believed that the ministry could survive on its own within five years! What lacked was a mutual giving and receiving; western missionaries had given financial and material resources, but they did not appear to accept and receive something back from the Kenyan people with whom they worked, such as their generosity, their hospitality, and their level of faith, such as Paul spoke about in Romans 15 (see Chapter One, pages 12-13).

Paul told the Church in Rome that because they had material and financial resources, they were indebted to give money to the financially poorer church in Jerusalem, who was rich in faith, but in need materially and financially. I believe Paul's economic instruction still applies today. Paul also wrote, *"Contribute your share with reference to the needs of the saints; give attention to hospitality"* (Romans 12:13 DNT). Missionaries and their supporting churches need to continue to follow Paul's instructions as found in the book of Romans.

Cultural Awareness and Respect

An ancient Chinese proverb said, *"If you want a definition of water, don't ask a fish"* (Newbigin, 1986, p. 21). In the context of missions, a missionary cannot just ask an indigenous person to explain their culture, since they live in it. Adequate preparation and study is essential so that missionaries will not do anything culturally disrespectful or offensive. I admit that I was not always adequately prepared for all that I would see, hear and experience, and I made several of my own blunders while in Kenya.

Missionaries must understand "contextualization," which is, *"Placing the gospel in the total context of a culture at a particular moment"* (Newbigin, 1986, p. 21). For example, many Africans have a deep sense of the spirit world and the supernatural. An effective missionary would not try to destroy those cultural beliefs, but rather channel them in the light of the gospel. Many Kenyans believe that there is a spirit world of deceased ancestors who oversee work in the home. If these ancestors were not buried with honor, they will come back and disturb the family through sickness, nightmares, or misfortunes, so they must be honored. However, the ancestors are honored and respected out of fear, and not out of love.

As Christians, we might assure the Kenyans who believe in ancestor worship that there is indeed a spirit world, but it consists of angels and the Holy Spirit, who casts out all fear and who has the power over death. Tradition is strong in Kenya concerning these ancestor beliefs, but missionaries can teach the indigenous people about God's power and His Spirit within their own traditions, thereby transforming their cultural beliefs through Christ.

Much of African culture also believes that spirits live in mountainous areas, in rivers, or in the wilderness. A missionary can reinforce these beliefs, but in the Christian context of the Bible. Biblical stories can be told depicting God's presence in these places, such as the Exodus story of the Israelites wandering in the wilderness, or Jesus going off to be alone in a quiet place (the wilderness), Jesus walking on the water, or calming the sea, baptisms in the rivers, etc.

A missionary can help remove the fear of the spirit world by explaining that since God is a spirit, and He lives inside of us through His Holy Spirit and He is present everywhere, including the mountains, the wilderness, and the rivers, that there is no need to fear. God is in complete control of the entire spiritual realm.

Instead of trying to completely change a culture that is viewed as heathen, a missionary can be culturally sensitive and find ways to use strong, cultural beliefs and traditions, and transform the culture through the message of Christ. (For a powerful example of this type of work that was done magnificently by a missionary, read, *The Peace Child: An Unforgettable Story of Primitive Jungle Treachery in the 20th Century* by Don Richardson, Regal Books, 2005). Roland Allen wrote concerning the African belief in the spirit world, *"Do not try to eradicate this belief and make a man hide from his beliefs in devils, which will make it even stronger, but instead, preach the supremacy of Christ as 'the real antidote,' a Savior who is there in their darkness"* (Allen, 1997, p. 29).

Another African tradition which missionaries in the past have not always handled correctly is polygamy. A man can have several wives for the purpose of being remembered by more people after his death, to own more property, to have more children, and sometimes just to satisfy his lust. Some Western missionaries have taught that once a man becomes a Christian, he must abandon all of his wives except one.

Unfortunately, when he abandoned the other wives, those women and children then viewed Christianity as an evil since it caused their abandonment.

The issue of polygamy caused a great deal of tension among missionaries. Some independent churches sanctioned the practice while other churches prohibited it entirely. Bishop Colenso startled everyone at the Lambeth Conference in 1860 by allowing this practice of polygamy. The Bishop said that requiring a man with multiple wives to keep only one in order to be baptized (which was a requirement at the time), was theologically inconsistent since it caused the man to, *"Commit the sin of divorce to remedy the offense of polygamy"* (Sanneh, 1989, p. 176). Today, most missionaries are not telling African men that the requirement for being Christian is to abandon some of his wives, but that they cannot take any more wives than they already have once becoming Christian.

Missionaries must see Christianity from other cultural perspectives. All believers need to comprehend and appreciate the great diversity God made in His creation, and the various ways He loves and reveals Himself in differing cultures. Many Asian and African Christians who have received the gospel from American missionaries *"struggle through their own study of scripture and their own obedience in their own time and place to articulate a form of Christian believing and behaving in terms of their own culture"* (Newbigin, 1986, p. 147). A culturally ignorant, arrogant or disrespectful missionary can therefore cause a great deal of confusion to a new believer.

Another point to remember in missions is that Christianity was culturally diverse from its earliest beginnings: Parthians, Medes, Elamites, Greeks and barbarians were all part of the community of believers when Christianity first began (Sanneh, 1989, p. 43). The Early Church shifted from Jerusalem to Antioch, and then from Europe to Asia to Africa. The Church has always been multi-cultural.

Cultural Problems in the Early Church

From its inception, the Christian Church has struggled with cultural diversity and with the concept of how Christians are supposed to live out their faith from culture to culture. In Acts chapter 15, we read of the famous Jerusalem Council, which met to decide how to deal with cultural issues: (Acts 15:1-29)

"But a group of men from Judea came to Antioch and taught the brethren, saying, Unless you are circumcised as Moses prescribed you cannot be saved. When Paul and Barnabas vigorously opposed them and questioned their teaching, it was determined that Paul and Barnabas and some of the group, should go to Jerusalem and discuss the question with the apostles and elders. The assembly sent them on their way and they passed through Phoenicia and Samaria, reporting the conversion of the Gentiles: this brought great rejoicing to the brotherhood. Arriving at Jerusalem, they were received by the congregation and the apostles and elders, and reported all that God had done. But certain of the converted Pharisees, said, that it was necessary to circumcise converts and to require them to keep the Law of Moses.

The apostles and elders came together to consider the question. After a heated discussion, Peter stood up and said, Brethren, you well know that in the past God made a choice that through my words the Gentiles should hear the gospel and learn to believe. And God who knows the hearts of men, gave evidence of this by bestowing on them the Holy Spirit just as He did on us; and God made no distinctions between us and them by cleansing their hearts by faith. Why do you now attempt to provoke God and put a yoke on believers which neither our fathers nor we were able to bear? But we believe that through the grace of the Lord Jesus Christ, we were saved just as they are.

They all kept silence and began to listen to Barnabas and Paul reporting what signs and miracles that God had performed through them among the Gentiles. And when they completed their report, James responded, saying, Brethren, listen to me: Simon has explained the way God at first visited the Gentiles to gather from them a people for His name. This is in full agreement with the words written by the prophets; there will come a time when I will return and rebuild the tent of David that has fallen down; and from the ruins I will set it up afresh: so that the rest of mankind might seek after the Lord, and all the Gentiles, among whom My name is called, said the Lord, whose work this is. God has known from the beginning what He does now. It is my judgment, therefore, that we do not further trouble those among the Gentiles who have turned to God: but that we send a written message that they abstain from food sacrificed to idols, from sexual immorality, from things strangled, and from tasting blood. For Moses has had in every city those who proclaim his Law for generations, because it is read aloud in the synagogues every Sabbath.

Then it seemed good to the apostles and elders, and the whole assembly, to send selected men from the congregation to Antioch with Paul and Barnabas; namely, Judas, called Barsabas, and Silas, who were leaders among the brethren: and the assembly sent a written message;

The apostles and elders and brethren send greetings to the Gentile brethren in Antioch, Syria, and Cilicia: since we have heard that some who came from us have disturbed you by teaching things not authorized by us: it seemed good, being assembled with one accord, to send chosen men to you with our beloved Barnabas and Paul; men who have risked their lives for the name of the Lord Jesus Christ. We have sent Judas and Silas, who shall confirm this message by their words. For it seemed good to the Holy Spirit and to us, not to impose any extra burden on you, apart from the necessary ones: that you abstain from food sacrificed to idols, from tasting blood, from things strangled, and from sexual immorality: if you guard against these things, you will be doing right. Be strong!" (Green, Acts 15:1-29 DNT)

The dilemma of Christ and culture existed almost immediately after the death and return of Jesus to Heaven, which we see in the Scripture above in the Jerusalem Council, and of course, this dilemma still exists today.

Global People

Missionaries must be "global people" who live in, "*more than one culture, have contact with more than one nation, prayed with disciples from more than one religion, learned more than one language, and are at home everywhere but not home anywhere*" (Bellagamba, 1992, p. 10). A missionary must also be able to move from one culture to another without feeling lost or confused, and accept multi-culturalism and multi-racism.

Anthony Bellagamba believed there are certain criteria for missionaries that included, but are not limited to, a deep spirituality, and a close relationship with God. The priority of a missionary should be to have God seen in them and in their lives. Another criterion is to act as a bridge builder between cultures and people, by understanding another culture's traditions, values, and language. A missionary should be able to develop various ministries as needed and be able and willing to adjust to different styles of worship and ministry. The final criterion is a concern for the poor and oppressed. Missionaries, "*must relearn the gospel and genuine humane values, including the ability to enjoy life in all its simplicity*" (Bellagamba, 1992, p. 9), and to partner with the poor for greater equality and justice.

Bellagamba also thinks that all missionaries need to go beyond themselves in order to understand and empathize with people living in totally different situations than from their own origins. A missionary must go beyond his or her own culture and appreciate and live in another culture. Missionaries need to learn about another culture's history, motivations, values, etc., and unlearn what they think is important and virtuous in order to appreciate another way of life. A missionary needs to learn the culture, the music, the dances and the language of the indigenous people and accept other forms of worship. A missionary needs to become a person of, "*dual citizenship, dual sets of values, dual understandings of reality, dual life and above all, dual culture"* (Bellagamba, 1992, p. 96).

This dualism should bring an understanding of differences in facts vs. values. While facts are a constant, values are not. For example, it is a *fact* that DNA is involved in our genetic makeup and in the development of all human beings, of any culture. However, it is a Christian *value* that human beings are created to glorify God and enjoy Him forever. Values involve personal choices, styles of living, divisions of labor, etc., which are reflected in both private and public life. A missionary who cannot separate facts from values can bring confusion and resentment to another culture. Unless a culture's values are completely contrary to Scripture (like the cattle raids and killing within the Pokot tribe), a globally minded missionary should not interfere.

Christ's teachings should encompass both public and private life, as He is Lord of every area of our lives. Sanneh wrote, *"A preaching of the gospel that calls men and women to accept Jesus as Savior but does not make it clear that discipleship means commitment to a vision of society radically different from that which controls our public life must be condemned as false"* (Sanneh, 1989, p. 200). Jesus is perceived differently from culture to culture, and a globally minded missionary will understand this and teach the Bible in light of the indigenous culture; in order to do this though, knowledge of the culture's traditions, values, and of course, language, is extremely important.

Language

Working and living in another culture, especially as a long term missionary, requires learning the language of the indigenous people. *"Language itself is a living expression of culture"* (Sanneh, 1989, p. 69), so in order to fully understand a culture, one must understand the language. However, understanding a language involves more than just understanding the actual words; it requires a full embodiment of a language. Most Kenyans speak English, but certain traditions and values need to be known to help explain an idea in Scripture. For example, some Kenyans will understand the concept of forgiveness if a missionary explains that they need to "present the neck," which is a custom in certain tribes where a person will bend down and show or present their neck, and they can either be forgiven, or have their head cut off. Even if the actual language or words are the same, to master the embodiment of a language requires actual understanding of the culture.

The Gospel of John is a wonderful example of fully understanding a language. Gnosticism was the religion of many of the people to whom John was writing, so he used Gnostic terminology to explain Jesus, such as the concepts of light and darkness. John's gospel is filled with Gnostic ideas and was written in a manner for the people to understand dualistic philosophy, which is central to Gnosticism.

Many of the apostles also had to use cultural interpretations and exegesis like the writer of the Gospel of John. Many of the disciples left their Jewish culture and entered Greek-speaking areas that not only spoke other languages, but also lived in different cultures. American missionaries need to remember that the Bible was of course, not written in English, and there are phrases, idioms and customs written in Scripture that are foreign to an American. The Bible was written in an eastern culture, thousands of years ago, and the ideas that are translated into English are not always understood without some knowledge of the history and culture in which it was written (for an excellent resource on Aramaic idioms, read, *Idioms in the Bible Explained and a Key to The Original Gospels* by George M. Lamsa, Harper Collins Publishers, 1985).

Translation of the Bible and the use of indigenous language are crucial so as not to exclude any people group from a, *"meaningful role in Christianity"* and to prevent any, *"foreign domination of the missionary culture"* (Sanneh, 1989, p. 108). Edwin Smith, who translated the New Testament in Zambia, said the following about the need for translation:

"Men need two kinds of language, in fact; a language of the home, of emotion, of unexpressed association; and a language of knowledge, steadfast in their meanings. Where the mother tongue does not answer both needs, the people must inevitably become bilingual; but however fluent they may succeed in being in the foreign speech, its words can never feel to them as their native words. To express the dear and intimate things which are the very breath and substance of life, a man will fall back on the tongue he learnt not in school, but in the house – how, he remembers not. He may bargain in the other, or pass examinations in it, but he will pray in his home speech. If you wish to reach his heart you will address him in his language" (Sanneh, 1989, p. 197).

One particular difficulty for missions in Africa is that there are so many languages and terms for God. Africans, on average, have always had a deep sense of the reality of God, but they confused missionaries because the missionaries were not sure what the indigenous people actually meant by "God." Because of cultural and language ignorance, many missionaries mistakenly believed that Africans had never heard of God. The "problem" in Africa was not too little religion, but actually too much religion! The language barrier often hindered missionaries, and made them incapable of understanding this "problem."

Literal word-for-word translation of an English Bible is insufficient into another language. For example, an English-speaking missionary cannot translate Isaiah 1:18 word for word for an African who does not speak English. This beautiful passage in Isaiah recorded, *"Come now, let us reason together says the Lord. Though your sins are as scarlet, they shall be white as snow, though they are red as crimson, they shall be like wool."* If an African has never seen snow, the phrase, "White as *snow*" will mean nothing. Instead, ideas need to be translated, and a missionary might translate that verse to say, "White as *milk*," in order to help the recipient culture understand.

Another example is the Karre people of Equatorial Africa. The Paraclete, or Comforter (the Holy Spirit), is called the, *"One who falls down beside you"* (Sanneh, 1989, p. 105). The Holy Spirit is understood as the person who accompanies, protects and sustains people on a journey since they have helpers who travel as companions through harsh and dangerous bush.

All of these examples stated above clearly show the need for cultural knowledge and culturally sensitive translations of Scripture. Cultural differences, understandings and sensitivity can be quite challenging, but adequate preparation, humility, and a teachable spirit can enable a missionary to be effective wherever God sends them. Once the cultural challenges have been understood, there remain some challenges of the Church to have effective mission's ministries.

Since I have long been interested in cultural diversity and the work of missions, I was interested in learning more about Kenya, about the role the Church can and should play in world missions and global Christianity, and in discovering our unique gifts that God wants to use if we allow ourselves to become a part of His larger story for the advancement of His kingdom. I knew there were many challenges and "Goliaths" in mission work and in living through cultural difficulties, but I was anxious to learn, share, and become more involved with SELIDEF, and in helping my local church catch the passion for God's work throughout the ends of the earth.

Lord, assist the Church and her people to overcome cultural differences that hinder the advance of Christianity!

KENYA

"What is the benefit, my cherished band of brothers, if a man says he has faith, and have not deeds?.... "

(James 2:14-18 DNT).

6

CHALLENGING THE CHURCH

An Alternative Perspective

One failure of some missionaries has been that they could gain many converts, often in large numbers, but they failed to train them to maintain their own spiritual life. St. Paul was effective in training leaders after he left the areas he visited; he planted many churches, but then he left and kept in contact only through letters and occasional visits. Mission work should be kind of a *"paternal relationship"* with the indigenous people, and then a *"coordinate position side by side"* with the missionaries and those people whom they came to serve (Sanneh, 1989, p. 144). Paul instructed his congregations through continuous communication, but not through direct, personal control and government.

Another mistake some missionaries have made was in their leadership. Missionaries sometimes educate and instruct their converts, but feel that only missionaries or appointed ministers can preach, for fear of theological mistakes. The indigenous people then hesitate to lead, preach and teach, and leave all of the responsibilities to the missionaries. In the past, American and European missionaries arrogantly believed that the African converts could not lead, but needed to depend on the missionaries for leadership. Many years ago the Episcopal Church said that, *"The African is not fit for the post of Bishop"* (Sanneh, 1989, p. 144). In response to this absurd statement, the Reverend James Johnson, assistant Bishop of Western Equatorial Africa, in 1900 said:

"Christianity is a religion intended for and is suitable for every race and tribe of people on the face of the globe. Acceptance of it was never intended by its Founder to denationalize any people and it is indeed its glory that every race of people may profess and practice it and imprint upon it its own native characteristics, giving it a peculiar type among themselves without losing anything of its value. And why should there not be an African Christianity as there has been a European and an Asiatic Christianity?" (Sanneh, 1989, p. 108).

While those of us today may think that the comment made by the Episcopal Church at that time does indeed sound ludicrous, this same attitude of superiority may still be present today, though in much more subtle and deceptive ways. For example, an American man, who for years was close friends with Nathan and a strong supporter of SELIDEF, pulled away from the ministry and ceased his friendship with Nathan and his wife. Nathan had no idea why this loss occurred, and he asked me to see what information I could uncover. When I returned to America after my last trip to Kenya, I called this man (since I had met him on several occasions in the past in Kenya). This American man said that when he first met Nathan and his wife, "They were living in a one-room shack and were the happiest people he had ever seen. Then, they began to become successful in their ministry and work, and they moved into a nice home, and therefore they had lost their core values."

After thinking about the comment this man made, I wondered what he meant by "losing their core values." Did he mean that Nathan, and all Kenyan Christians, should always remain poor, which is what this man implied? I was unsure of what he meant, so to clarify his statement, I later emailed him and asked how he justified Americans working hard and improving their standard of living, which is applauded and respected, but when a poor Kenyan does the same thing, he has lost his "core values." I never did receive a response. While our cultural arrogance may not be as ignorant as it was in the past, it has not completely been removed either.

On World Missions Day in 1989, the Pope made the following statement: *"Whoever is in charge of the mission must be primarily concerned about good formation of the indigenous clergy, in which rests the greatest hope of the new Christian community"* (Bellagamba, 1992, p. 46).

My good friend Kibii, the former program director of a seminary in Kenya, said that the Kenyans welcome American missionaries because they bring a different perspective on some ideas. Kibii believes the exchange of Americans and Kenyans is a helpful, healthy, and positive experience for both groups of people since they are exposed to one another's cultures, values and thoughts. This exchange of culture is crucial for the life of the Church as Christ intended, but unfortunately, this exchange is often resisted.

The Local American Church

Many churches in America, especially in small towns and rural areas, are often resistant to helping people outside of their respective communities. I have lived in many different states in America, including large cities and major metropolitan areas like my hometown of Chicago, but I have also lived in various small towns and rural areas as well. I realized that the way of life and the ways of thinking are often quite different from cities to rural areas, but I also wondered how the gospel message can be more widely presented in whatever type of setting one resides. For example, at a wonderful, small, rural church that I am presently a member of, the practice of global missionary work was non-existent. The church had no mission board, they did not sponsor or send out any missionaries, and the church had little outreach to people other than to the people in the county of which this church resided, and that outreach did not always involve evangelism. Having come from churches that have always had strong mission and evangelism focuses, I was surprised at the mission void in this church.

In my attempt to understand my new church, I spoke to several long-time church members, who said they felt they should focus their help on people within their own church and town and primarily in physical ways, without necessarily mentioning Jesus. I did not know if this way of thinking was indicative of most of the members, but I did come to realize that there were other people in this church who did share these views. I thought of something I once read that prompted my desire for a vision of global outreach and mission work within our church: *"But it's (the Church) essential core remained: within the community of believers there can never be room for a poverty that denies anyone what is needed for a dignified life"* (Pope Benedict XVI, *God is Love*, 2006, p. 54). I thought of the word "anyone" to include my friends in Kenya and those who lived anything but a dignified life in most Third World countries, which are so vastly different from America. The *"community of believers"* is also world-wide.

After speaking to Steve, the senior pastor of my church, and his wife and associate pastor Jyn, and two other people in the church who also had a passion for missions (Phillip and Grace), we decided to begin the challenging task of bringing a global vision to our congregation that would move beyond our church walls and community. We hoped to bring more life and excitement to our small church and expand the church's concept of God, the Christian faith, and our obligation as Christians to live out the Great Commission.

For many months, pastor Steve, his wife Jyn, Phillip, Grace and I met to discuss how and what our mission vision might look like in this church, and where we would even begin. I met with pastors Steve and Jyn several times to share the hope of my vision, which comprised the following ideas: incorporate a percentage of the church budget for missions, which would include assisting the pastors and members of the church to go abroad on short term mission trips, have a *"Missions Month"* each year, where each sermon in that month would speak about mission work, have an annual Missions Conference, with experienced missionary speakers, and display pictures and items that people had from previous mission trips, host an international pot luck dinner, and eventually send out our own full time missionary who would emerge from our church. My pastor and his wife were eager to try. I spoke to Phillip and Grace about these ideas, and we were all excited!

The Work Began

Phillip, Grace and I got together several times to share ideas, and since I was new to the church and they were long time members, their help was invaluable. We knew we needed a detailed policy and budget to present to the various committees and boards that many American churches have, but we did not know how to craft these documents. My former church has a large mission focus, and they have a Missions/Administrative pastor, named Glenn, who we thought might be able to help get us started. I contacted Glenn to ask for his help, and he said he would pray about it and of course ask his boss, the senior pastor, Steve, to see what he would say (so as not to confuse the reader, both pastors are named Steve - from my former and my current church). Steve gave a resounding "go" to Glenn, and said that if one church can help another in growing the Kingdom of God, he would be happy to help. I was impressed with the openness of Pastor Steve to share their church's' knowledge and experience with another church, without any sense of competition which unfortunately accompanies many churches, leaders and ministries.

We asked if Glenn and his wife Linda could come out to our church for a weekend, in order to meet together with our newly formed mission board (Grace, Phillip, Pastor Steve and me), and with the pastor and his wife Jyn. We wanted Glenn to help us begin launching a global vision of missions to our church, and to speak on the first Sunday of our *"Missions Month"* that we were planning for the month of August. Glenn agreed to come and speak, and Pastor Steve agreed to let

Glenn give up a weekend of work at his own church to assist our church.

I was most grateful for the generous spirit of love, partnership and selfless giving that my former church held. We planned for Glenn and Linda to come to our little town and to have dinner with us at Phillip and Grace's house, share what their church was doing with mission work, spend the night at Phillip and Grace's house, and speak at the two services in our church the following morning. Our hopes were high as we prayed to help our congregation gain a passion for missions and a vision of the global church.

The Arrival

Glenn and Linda arrived and settled into their new home for the weekend, with the pastor and his wife arriving shortly thereafter. Everyone quickly became friends as we sat in Phillip and Grace's beautiful living room and shared stories. I was delightfully surprised at all of the information Glenn brought, and how transparent his church was in sharing their knowledge with us. Glenn brought the church's full, detailed missions policy, their budget, and their complete disclosure of funds. He shared the names, pictures and information about each missionary their church supports and the amount of financial support each receives from the church. Glenn brought magazines we could subscribe to, books and a DVD missions class with accompanying books for teaching about the work of missions, called *Operation WorldView,* which I highly suggest as an introductory course. I was familiar with this course since I took it when I was a member at Glenn and Linda's church just a few of years ago.

After dinner we took Glenn and Linda to the church so they could set up, and also to allow Glenn to see where he would be preaching. Glenn said he had experienced an unusual amount of fear, anxiety and various troubles this week in preparing for this weekend trip, and he even started to reconsider! We all knew it was the Enemy (Satan), attempting to stop our church from becoming a mission-minded, global church, alive and on fire for Jesus. Good things were sure to come.

Missions Kick Off

We were all excited to begin *Missions Month* at our little church, and when Glenn got up to speak, all fear and anxiety left him, and he spoke calmly, with gentleness and a good sense of humor. Glenn's Scriptural text was Acts 1:8,

"But you shall receive miraculous ability and strength after the Holy Spirit is come upon you; and you shall be my witnesses unto the death both in Jerusalem, and in all Judea, and in Samaria, and continually unto the farthest parts of the earth" (Acts 1:8 DNT).

The congregation was attentive and appeared interested. Glenn shared his passion and love for mission work, as he has taken over thirty short term mission trips around the world. Glenn spoke about the 10/40 window (the area of the world located between 10 and 40 degrees north of the equator), which is considered unreached, with people groups who still need to hear the Gospel of Jesus Christ. Many of the countries in this 10/40 window are Muslim, and evangelizing can often be dangerous.

Glenn also spoke about what is called the 4/14 window, which is the age group most receptive to the Gospel, and the ages where most people come to Christ. Glenn's emphasis on the 4/14 window is for mission work to include children's outreach, such as Vacation Bible Schools, Sunday Schools, and any ministry that reaches children. Glenn shared touching stories and pictures of his mission trips, and the connections and relationships he made with people he went to serve over the years, with an emphasis on putting a face to the word "missions."

Glenn spoke about the need for evangelizing within our own communities, but also about stretching ourselves and going outside of our comfort zones. Cross-cultural work, according to Glenn (and myself) changes our lives, builds our faith, and gives us a broader perspective on God, on people's needs, on how we live, including how we spend our money, on evangelizing, and on the Church in general. God breaks our hearts through mission work and makes us more sensitive to the needs of others. There were also examples of what a missionary might go and do, such as children's ministries, sewing classes, construction work, worship services, including singing, playing an instrument and dancing (depending on the culture), medical missions, feeding centers, cooking, and of course teaching and preaching. Everyone has some gift that can be utilized in mission work.

Included in Glenn's presentation were some funny and adventurous pictures, to show the congregation some of the added benefits God gives when working as a missionary. One important concept Glenn emphasized was the need to build relationships with people cross-culturally, to gain another's trust, and then to present the gospel. With the various types of ministries that Glenn mentioned as examples of mission work, relationships would flow naturally while working with the indigenous people.

Mission work is always reciprocal; we should never go to some other country with the attitude that we will help the people, feel good about ourselves, and leave. We should go out in order to get to know other people and cultures, develop loving and trusting relationships, and then share the Gospel of Jesus Christ. Glenn challenged our church to consider the need for mission work, and to incorporate a mission budget, plan, and policy for our church. Glenn's presentation was warmly accepted, and our church appeared to have made a positive connection to Glenn's church, which is what mission work is really all about.

The Great Commission

The following Sunday Phillip preached on the Scriptural mandate for missions by using the final words of Jesus as He left the earth, known as the *"Great Commission."*

"As you personally go, (going) therefore, and make disciples of all nations, baptizing them in the name of the Father, and of the Son, and of the Holy Spirit: teaching them to observe all things whatever I have commanded you" (Matthew 28:19-20a DNT).

Phillip emphasized that mission work (making disciples) is not an option for the Church, but a command given by Jesus, in order for all people throughout the world to hear about Him, and to have the opportunity for salvation in Christ alone. Phillip said that God does not have a "plan B!" The focus of the sermon was to think, act, serve, and love outside of our own church walls. Americans live quite comfortably compared to the rest of the world, so American Christians need to share their time, their talents, and their money to assist others, rather than focus on their own needs. Phillip said far too many churches "feed themselves" and focus on their own needs, rather than focus on the needs of others. The American Church, and our church in specific, can, and must reach out to other areas in need with the Good News of Jesus Christ, in addition to meeting the tangible needs of others. One way to accomplish this task is to tithe the church budget for missions.

Phillip's sermon was entitled, *"Trust and Obey."* If the Bible tells us to tithe, and God promises to provide for our needs when we do tithe, then the church should also tithe their budget for missions, and trust God to pay the bills each month. The American church is often basically, "American civic religion," which acts, thinks and lives no differently than the rest of the world, and often lacks faith. Does God bless our country and many of us personally, with abundance to spend on ourselves, or to serve and give to others? The challenge for individual Christians, as well as for churches, is to really trust God, and obey the final words of Jesus when He left this earth, to go into all the world and make disciples. Jesus' own disciples were ordinary, simple, uneducated men, yet they were entrusted with the gospel message to go into the world with the power of the Holy Spirit. Many of us in the church are simple, ordinary people, but we too can go into the entire world through God's Holy Spirit, if we would only trust Him.

How do American Christians define themselves? Do we think we are following Christ because of what we do *not* do, or by what we do? For example, how many church-going people think they are Christian because they do not drink, smoke, kill, steal, etc.? Did Jesus not define His followers by what they actively did, like trust, obey, serve, and make disciples of all people throughout the world? Where is our focus? Is it on us and our own comforts, or is it on the lost, the desperate, the poor and those who do not yet know Jesus?

Philip is a retired doctor and has been involved in medical missions in Colombia for several years with his wife Grace. Their passion lies in assisting the poor people of the earth, particularly Colombians, in meeting their medical needs, preventing them from dying from treatable diseases, and then sharing the Gospel and love of Jesus Christ with those whom he serves.

Paul's Admonishment

The third Sunday of our *Mission's Month* was my turn to preach, and I spoke primarily on the importance of mission work. I began with a powerful message from John Piper as found on a video that was shown at the 2010 Lausanne Mission Conference, which can be seen on U Tube, called, *"Tears of the Saints"* (I highly recommend watching this video, which can be found by typing in the given title along with John Piper's name on U Tube). John Piper said we have the three options when it comes to mission work that I mentioned in chapter one: we can go ourselves to another land as a missionary, we can send others out, supporting and praying for them, or we can disobey God. There simply are no other options.

I spoke of the need to assist other churches and ministries across the ocean, and the need to reach the people who do not know Jesus through first meeting their physical needs. Missionaries need to first help people feel loved and important, develop trusting relationships, and *then* spread the Gospel of Jesus Christ. My Scriptural text was Romans 15:23-29,

"Previously I have been hindered from coming to you. But now since the work here is completed, and having a great desire for many years to come to you; when I travel to Spain, I will visit you: for I hope to include you in my journey and be aided forward after I have enjoyed your company for a while. But first I must go to Jerusalem to deliver a collection to the saints. For the provinces of Macedonia and Achaia have freely made a contribution for the poor saints in Jerusalem. It was a pleasure for the Gentiles, being debtors and partakers of spiritual things, to feel responsible to minister in material things. When I have finished this task and assured the delivery of the collection, I plan to visit you on my way to Spain. And I am certain that when I visit you it will be in the fullness of the blessing of the gospel of Christ" (Romans 15:22-29 DNT).

I challenged our wealthier American church to help SELIDEF, a struggling and poor ministry in Kenya, East Africa, and my friend Nathan who runs that ministry, in the same manner that Paul instructed the wealthier churches in Greece to assist the poorer churches in Jerusalem. I challenged our church to partner with Nathan and SELIDEF to help transform the lives of the poor communities in rural Kenya through the provision of solar lamps, stoves, clean water, orphanages and the Gospel of Jesus Christ. I shared some pictures of my last trip to Kenya, and some of the people involved in SELIDEF, as well as pictures of the remote villages that SELIDEF serves. My hope was to share the joy of building relationships with people across the world, and the beauty of multi-culturalism in the Church, as well as to show the dire needs of so many people in the world in ways we cannot even imagine from the comforts of our American homes.

Additional Scriptures that were used in my sermon included *The Great Commission* in Matthew 28:18-20, which again, explains the biblical mandate for missions in the words of Jesus just before He ascended into Heaven. Another Scripture that I used to talk about the need to help our brothers and sisters across the ocean was 1 John 3:16-18,

"God manifested his love to us by laying down his life for our sakes; we too must be ready to lay down our lives for the sakes of the brothers. But whoso has more worldly goods than he needs, and sees his brother in need, and closes up his heart to compassion, how does the love of God reside in him? My little children, do not let love be in word or unnatural language, but in a true test of action" (1 John 3:16-18 DNT).

As I thought about helping the poor rural Kenyans that SELIDEF reaches out to with simple items such as solar lamps, cooking stoves and clean water, I found this Scripture in 1 John to be quite applicable.

The next Scriptural text came from James 2:14-18,

"What is the benefit, my cherished band of brothers, if a man says he has faith, and have not deeds? Can faith save him? If a brother or a sister is destitute of daily necessities, and has no clothing, of what use is it to say to the needy, 'Come in and be warmed, eat all you can and depart in peace;' although you give them none of the essentials which are needful to the body? Even so faith without praiseworthy deeds is like an unburied corpse left alone. Yes, a man may affirm that he has faith, and not have deeds; show me your faith apart from deeds, and I will show you faith by my deeds" (James 2:14-18 DNT).

We are all held accountable for the things we know, and if we choose to ignore the needs of others, both spiritually and physically, we will one day have to explain to God why we looked the other way. Our local church has a beautiful building for worship, we all have homes with running water, heat and electricity, and most of us have cars to get wherever we need to go. We have far more than the basic necessities, and far more than we actually need.

In America, we also have access to television, radio, all forms of print media such as newspapers, magazines, and the Internet, and there are multiple churches in every town, all of which enable us to have easy access of the Gospel. Many Third World countries, especially in rural areas, have no access to any of these ways to hear the Gospel, and therefore they have no way to hear about Jesus. We need to go to these places to tell them the good news of salvation.

The people in Kenya that SELIDEF serves live in rural, isolated areas, and they do not have access to television, radios, movies or the Internet, and therefore they do not have the chance to hear about Jesus and the Gospel message of salvation. Unless we send people out to tell these rural Kenyans about Christ, how will they know? Also, how much easier would it be for Kenyans to understand that there is a God who knows them intimately and who loves them, when their lives are being improved, their children and families are protected and better cared for, and their daily, tangible needs are better met? We as Christians can form relationships and friendships across cultures because of the love of Jesus, and we can share Jesus' command of serving one another as the Body of Christ.

I challenged our little church to intentionally and sacrificially live according to scripture as a global church, which is what Christ intended the Church to be, and to partner with brothers and sisters across the oceans, who are poor in material things, but rich in faith. I personally do not want to miss out on what God is doing across the world, and I want to join Him in the privilege of being used for the building of His Kingdom. God wants to bring us along and join Him in His work, if only we are willing. What part of God's story do you want to be in? God wants to write us into His marvelous plan of salvation. The Bible says the harvest is plentiful, but the workers are few, and again, I think of John Piper's message: "Go, send, or disobey."

Perfect Love

The fourth Sunday of our *Missions Month*, Jyn, the pastor's wife, who is also the Associate Pastor of the church, spoke on James 1:27,

"Free from all that would dim the transparency in belief and conduct before God the Father is this, to go and see and relieve the orphans without a father's protection and the women lacking a husband in their distress, and to keep himself untainted with guilt" (James 1:27 DNT).

Jyn has been involved in a Christian orphanage in Haiti for several years now, but has not yet traveled to this place. Jyn expressed a desire to go there, with others from the congregation, and also have the church support this orphanage in prayer and in finances. Jyn spoke of the wonderful opportunity that exists for us to show "perfect love" to these orphans, and generate an interest in caring for these children who simply need love. The orphanage that Jyn spoke about is transparent with their financial records and can be trusted with any money that we send. The orphanage also teaches the children about Jesus, and cares not only for the physical needs of the children, but their spiritual needs as well.

The Basin, the Pitcher, and the Towel

Our fifth and final sermon on missions was delivered by the senior pastor who wrapped up *Missions Month* at our church. He spoke about serving, and used the example of Jesus washing His disciple's feet as spoken of in John 13:1-17,

"Before the Festival of the Passover, Jesus knew that the hour had come that He should leave this world and return to the Father, having loved His own in the world, Jesus showed love for them to the end. And supper being in process, the devil having now put into the heart of Judas Iscariot, Simon's son, to betray Jesus; knowing that the Father had given all things into His hands, and that He came from God, and went to God; Jesus rose from supper, and laid aside His garments; and took a towel, and girded Himself. Then He poured water into a

container, and began to wash the disciples' feet, and to wipe them with the towel about His waist. Then Jesus approached Simon Peter and Peter asked, Lord, do you wash my feet? Jesus answered, What I do you do not understand now; but you will later. Peter said, You will never wash my feet. Jesus answered, Unless I wash you, you will have no part with Me. Simon Peter said to Him, Lord, not my feet only, but also my hands and my head. Jesus said, He who is bathed need to wash only his feet, but is complete clean: and you are clean, but not all. For Jesus knew who would betray Him; therefore He said, You are not all clean.

So after washing their feet, Jesus put on His robe and returned to the table, and asked, Do you understand what I have done to you? You call Me Master and Lord: and you are correct; because I AM. If I then, your Lord and Master, have washed your feet; you ought to willingly wash one another's feet. I have given you an example that you should do as I have done to you. Truly, I say, The slave is not greater than his master; neither is a messenger sent greater than the one who sent him. If you know these things, blessed are you if you do them. (John 13:1-17 DNT).

Pastor Steve spoke about the importance of humbly serving others as Jesus commanded us to do by His own example, with the basin, the pitcher and the towel. We are to love and to serve all people everywhere, which is the basis of missions. Missionaries must go out with humble hearts and be willing to love and serve others in many ways, including caring for the sick in Colombia, bringing simple conveniences to rural Kenyans, along with good biblical teaching, and caring for orphans, all while also bringing people hope through the Good News of the Gospel of Jesus Christ.

Missions Month

We ended the first ever "Missions Month" with five weeks of sermons about the importance and the joy of missions, in hopes of getting the congregation excited and interested in taking their own mission trips. Many people in the church are financially comfortable, and we hoped to give them a broader vision of the Church of Jesus Christ and the work of the Kingdom through mission work. Our new missions group was hoping to gain some financial support for our ministries in Colombia, Kenya and Haiti, and also to get financial assistance for people to go on mission trips to these locations, and like Pastor Glenn said, to put a face to the word "missions." We also knew that if we could get our own pastor overseas on a short term mission trip, that his enthusiasm for a strong mission focus in the church would be born.

Lord, give the Church and her people a vision for missions!

~

"Mission work is always reciprocal; we should never go to some other country with the attitude that we will help the people, feel good about ourselves, and leave."

7

DEVELOPING A MISSIONS POLICY

The Next Step

The next step was to work on a mission policy to present to the Outreach Committee, the Elders, and then to the Cabinet, which consisted of the Chairs of all the ministries in the church. Because our small, rural church did not presently have a strong mission or global focus, we thought we needed to be quite detailed in what the vision was for incorporating mission work into our church.

Phillip, Grace and I worked off of the model Glenn left us from his church, and tailored it to fit our church. Glenn's help was invaluable, and with this detailed, cohesive policy, we felt fairly confident that our church would embrace our vision to the extent of at least making this policy a part of the church. We wanted to give Scriptural mandates for mission work, what our concept of missions would look like for our church, and how the new mission program would be budgeted and incorporated into our church.

Here is the policy that any church is free to use, and which our church adapted from Glenn's church. The policy is printed here with permission by Glenn, his church, Steve and my church:

A. Biblical Basis of Missions

Those who know Christ, can, and must love and serve the world as He loves and serves us. This is clearly spelled out in Matthew 28:18-20, I John 3:16-18, James 2:14-18, Romans 15:23 and Romans 15:23-28.

B. Missions and the Church

FCC (I will refer to my church as FCC), exists for the glory of God and for missions. We follow the active leadership of God's Holy Spirit in our choice of mission's involvement for FCC. We cite the church at Antioch as our model in this.

1. We consider prayer the initial tool in missions outreach, bringing God's power and resources into our church and world.

2. Missions should be central to our existence as a church. Our involvement in missions shall require sacrifice in other areas, both corporately and individually.

3. We support missions out of an intense desire to worship and to serve God, and to see the salvation of men, women, children, people groups, and nations.

C. Strategy for Missions Outreach

1. We purpose to love and serve the world through mission activity in three focused outreach areas:

a. Developing indigenous church workers in reached countries, internationally

b. Targeting unreached people

c. National missions

2. In order to do this, FCC members need to be:

a. Missions Prayer Warriors

b. Missions Faith Givers

c. Active Team Members

d. Students of Missions

3. Mission Planning Group (MPG) members should lead the way in missions by their:

a. Involvement in missions work nationally and /or internationally

b. Active prayer for discernment of God's plan for FCC missions outreach

c. Openness to being called into full-time missions work

d. Personal involvement in mobilizing the FCC body to develop a love for missions

e. Taking the *Operation WorldView* course and be prepared to teach this course

f. Planning and executing regular missions exposure for FCC

4. We see this "regular mission's exposure" as taking such forms as:

a. Annual Missions Conference / Celebration / Weekend

b. Annual International Dinner

c. Quarterly Missions Sundays

d. Weekly Visibility of FCC involvement in missions

e. Encouraging the congregation to be involved in Praying, Giving, and Going for world missions

f. Seek to support, in part, at least one full time missionary.

g. Recommending the assignment of individual missionaries to small Groups (Sunday School classes, Shepherding Flocks, etc.), for mutual encouragement, prayer, and correspondence

h. Promoting and / or teaching the *Operation WorldView* course

i. Inviting missionaries and other mission mobilizers to speak to the church or Small Groups to further promote a world vision among our members.

j. Essentially anything that helps to develop the body of FCC into "World Christians"*

* A World Christian is someone who is so gripped by the glory of God and the glory of His global purpose that he/she chooses to align himself with God's mission to fill the earth

with the knowledge of His glory as the waters cover the sea (Habakkuk 2:14). [David Bryant has helped define and popularize the notion of "World Christian" in his book In the Gap; Intervarsity Press, 1979]

5. MPG members will perform the following administrative tasks:

    a. Compile the annual missions budget

    b. Recommend to the Elders, then the Finance Committee the annual disbursement of the budget

    c. Correspond with missions boards concerning the support of their (future) personnel

    d. Approve support requests for long and short-term missionaries, organizations, ministries, and projects

    e. Participate on ad hoc committees designated by the MPG

D. MPG Membership

The MPG shall be comprised of a minimum of three and no more than seven voting individuals, and one non-voting member of the Pastoral Staff. All of the above mentioned shall either be members or have been regular attendees for a minimum of 12 months and be in good standing with FCC. Only FCC members would be eligible for the leadership positions of Chairperson, Vice Chairperson, and Secretary.

QUORUM – A majority of persons, 2/3, qualified to vote shall constitute a quorum. For the purpose of constituting a quorum, an MPG member must be present at the meeting in person or as described below. An MPG member shall be deemed to be present at a meeting for the purpose of constituting a quorum, and transacting business thereof, if, at the time of such meeting, he/she shall participate by telephone in the transaction of the business thereof.

A quorum would also consist of a majority of persons qualified to vote, transacting business of support issues for "short term" requests, when necessary, by email and/or telephone prior to the next regularly scheduled meeting. The majority vote of the quorum shall constitute a majority vote of the board.

1. Members:

a. Membership duration: 3 years with option for one consecutive renewable term.

b. Rotation: 1/3 rotating off each year after the initial MPG at the end of the church calendar year

c. Selection: from a list of potential members nominated and approved by the MPG in December or when vacancies occur due to member circumstances.

d. Responsibility: to serve in accordance to Scripture.

2. Officers:

A. Chairperson

   1. Duration: 1 to 3 years

   2. Selection: made by the MPG membership subject to review and confirmation by the Board of Elders and the Senior Pastor.

   3. Responsibility: to provide leadership and structure of meetings, designate assigned duties; work closely with the pastor of missions and / or senior pastor on mission's strategy, focus, and concern, and to ensure accountability and the execution of assigned tasks with proper follow-up.

B. Vice-Chairperson:

   1. The responsibilities of the vice-chair are to preside over MPG meetings if the chairperson is unavailable and to serve on the executive committee whose responsibilities are outlined below.

C. Treasurer/Accountant:

   1. The MPG accounts shall be handled by the church treasurer through Outreach Ministry. The MPG is currently a sub-committee of Outreach. When the bylaws are revised, MPG and Outreach will be two separate ministries. The missions fund will be part of one general fund bank account. Breakdown for specific funds (e.g. general, building, missions, etc.) are all separated on paper only.

2. In addition to annual budgeting allowances to the MPG fund, at the end of the church calendar year, undistributed MPG funds will be carried forward in the MPG accrual account.

E. Secretary:

1. Duration: 1 to 3 years

2. Selection: made by the MPG on the first month of the calendar year

3. Responsibility: to take minutes of each meeting, distribute the minutes to the MPG members and Cabinet, and facilitate communication between the MPG chairperson, MPG members, pastors, Elders, (future) supported missionaries, and mission organizations.

F. Missions Prayer Coordinator:

1. The Missions Prayer Coordinator will be responsible for organizing and facilitating intercessory prayer for the MPG, MPG meetings, and its missionaries (See Appendix A).

2. Duration – 1 to 3 years

G. Methods of Program Evaluation

The MPG Committee will make an annual review of MPG goals and actions during the budget development process in the Fall. A member of the pastoral staff will assist in the evaluation. The following will be taken into consideration in the evaluation:

1. Biblical basis for missions focus

2. Allocation of funds in keeping with guidelines, strategy, and areas of focus

3. Effectiveness of the missions program as measured by:

-Attendance at missions functions

-Amount of mission's faith promise and mission's budget

-FCC member's commitment to missionary service

-Weekly prayer support for missions

H. Future Guidelines for Missions Support

FCC, through the collective "faith promises" (pledges made by the congregation of additional giving specifically for missions), of the congregation and a percentage of the general fund, will financially support missions, subject to the following guidelines:

1. Types of Ministries

Missionaries, ministries or projects in the U.S. or foreign countries will be considered for support if in accordance with FCC mission strategies and goals: currently for example, FCC's summer youth mission trips, Haiti, Colombia, and Kenya. The majority of support will be budgeted for the support of missionaries. Each ministry considered shall demonstrate measurable goals and accountability of tasks performed.

2. Priority Emphasis for Funding

- Members of FCC who answer God's call to missionary service under any organization acceptable to FCC will be considered first. Priority will then be given to missionary support candidates that meet the following criteria:
- must be a member of FCC for one (1) year before being considered eligible for support
- demonstrated an active role in ministry at FCC
- active in their involvement in missions mobilization at FCC
- served or assisted MPG with its work
- shown a noticeable commitment to evangelism and outreach at home and abroad
- been a faithful participant in missions at FCC
- shown overall maturity and holiness in their Christian walk as seen through those that know them best

3. Amount of support

Support amounts are governed by the following stipulations for future consideration:

- Long Term Missionaries / overseas:

*FCC active members – a maximum of $300/month/single and $500/month/couple

- Short termers / overseas (3 months to 1 year):

*FCC active members – amount will generally not exceed $200/month for the length of term or $2400 one time amount

Short termers / homeland or overseas (less than 3 months):

*FCC members – eligible for up to $250 one time amount annually.

- Pastoral Staff Missions Trips:

To encourage the mission's vision at FCC it is vital that the pastoral staff lead the way in their mission involvement. The MPG will attempt to support full time pastoral staff of FCC on one trip per year at a maximum of $800. The pastoral staff will be governed by the same criteria concerning funding for long and short-term missionaries.

At the discretion of the MPG, the committee can approve amounts over the $800 maximum if the Senior Pastor is participating in a mission effort that would require him or her to travel more than once in a given year, or if a single trip requires additional funding above and beyond the allotted $800.

Operation WorldView:

Operation WorldView is an internationally renowned study program developed by the U.S. Center for World Mission.

The MPG feels this course is a valuable training tool to equip the body to stay on the "cutting edge" of what God is doing in the world today from a biblical, historical, cultural, and strategic perspective, and is required for consideration for funding.

- Non-Budgeted Project Support:

During the course of the budget year opportunities may arise to give to a ministry or special need that fits in with FCC mission's strategy and focus. The MPG can approve gift amounts up to a maximum of $500. This type of request can be granted no more than twice for the same person or ministry in each calendar year.

- Important Clarifications:

*All membership requirements based on a minimum of one year and active involvement in the church.

* All applicants for support may be asked to interview with the MPG.

*Support amounts will be based on availability of funds and criteria above.

*The MPG will not approve support amounts less than $50 per month.

*Long Term Support will not be considered until the budget planning meeting held after the Mission Conference in November of each year.

4. Start and Length of Support (applicable to Long Term Missionaries)

Support may be requested by missionaries to begin no more than three months prior to their expected date of departure for their field of service. If the departure date is delayed the missionary must report to the MPG before the end of the 4th month with an explanation of the delay and a report on the new timetable for departure. Based on that report the MPG may suspend or extend the support for another three months at which point the MPG will request another update.

A missionary's term will be supported for a period of up to five years after which time the support renewal may be subject to review.

5. Continuation and renewal of support

At the end of the term of service or change in assignment or affiliation, or leaving the mission field, the church's commitment will be subject to review and may be continued, renewed or canceled.

6. Organizational limitations

In order to maintain a worldwide and multifunctional vision, support of any organization's program should not exceed thirty-five percent (35%) of the total mission budget. This would not apply to individual missionaries serving in the same organization.

7. Homeland / Overseas ratio

The total amount spent locally in comparison to non-local and overseas should not exceed a 1/3 – 2/3 ratio respectively.

8. Visitation requirement

It is expected that support will be given to persons having close ties to FCC. It is desirable when the missionary is home on furlough for the missionary to spend significant time at FCC and any other supporting churches, in order to be nurtured, and help to raise the mission consciousness of FCC and the other churches. Prayer support, correspondence, and accountability will be monitored. The responsibility is, in turn, FCC's to encourage and help the congregation visit our missionaries on the field in order to foster an atmosphere of "co-laboring".

Missionaries will be apprised of policy when granted support, e.g. to maintain regular contact with MPG;

Support will be reviewed after 5 years of service.

I. Initial Ministry Goals

Initial annual support: "God's Littlest Angels," in Haiti, Colombia Medical Missions, and SELIDEF in Kenya of $1500. each as a love offering, with expectations of FCC members/pastoral staff traveling to visit these ministries as frequently as time and expenses allow.

1. $800. per year for pastoral staff travel expenses
2. $2400. Annually for a future potential full time missionary
3. $1000. Annually for travel expenses for short term missionaries

MPG PRAYER STRATEGY

FCC Prayer Force

Mission Division

Mission: The FCC Prayer Force will provide prayer cover and protection for FCC missionaries fighting the battle on the ground in the spiritual war as described in Ephesians 6:10-18.

Implementation: Include a Mission Prayer Coordinator as an office in the MPG. The Prayer Coordinator will be responsible for organizing and facilitating intercessory prayer for the MPG, MPG meetings, and its missionaries.

MPG Monthly Meetings: Set aside agenda time at each meeting to spend an intentional prayer time to seek God's presence and guidance for our planning, as well as other specific mission needs-including intentional listening time. The Prayer Coordinator will plan and facilitate this prayer time.

Prayer Unit: Organize a Prayer Unit to provide prayer cover and protection for each individual missionary. Each unit will be assigned one missionary. A MPG member (or others as needed) will serve as a prayer unit leader for an intercessor group. The MPG prayer unit leader will plan, organize and lead the group in seeking God on behalf of their designated missionary. The Leader will provide leadership for communicating with the missionary to determine prayer needs and to send encouragement to their specific missionary (when appropriate). The Leader will report their group's activity, successes and needs each month at the MPG meeting.

Church-wide Prayer: Continue FCC's email communication of specific missionary prayer needs to the MPG. When appropriate, put missionary prayer needs on the Church's weekly prayer email list. Include a prayer emphasis/event/time in connection with the annual Mission's Conference. Other initiatives will be added as needed and appropriate.

Children Praying for Children: Children's/youth programs and the children and youth in Sunday School classes, will be asked to pray for the children of the Haitian orphanage, the children of Columbia, the children of Kenya, and eventually children of our missionaries. Children will also be asked to pray for their supported child in Haiti. Involving the children in prayer will help them to grow with the understanding of the importance of missions, and the need for prayer within mission work.

Our Hopes for Our Church

I was hopeful that all of our work to bring about a global vision to our church and to create an interest and love for missions was beginning to take hold; for some people, it did. Some other people though, continued to ask why we did all of the work that we did, and why we feel missions is so important. The answer is quite simple: a love for all people and a desire to obey Jesus Christ.

Pope Benedict XIV wrote about the Church in the following words, which I feel summarizes our philosophy of mission work and why we desired to implement a global vision to our church:

> "Following the example given in the parable of the Good Samaritan, Christian charity is first of all the simple response to immediate needs and specific situations: feeding the hungry, clothing the naked, caring for and healing the sick, visiting those in prison, etc" ...Christians need to dedicate themselves to others with heartfelt concern, enabling them to experience the richness of their humanity...and the need to be led to that encounter with God in Christ which awakens their love and opens their spirits to others. As a result, love of neighbor will no longer be for them a commandment imposed, so to speak, from without, but a consequence deriving from their faith which becomes active through love" (Pope Benedict XVI, 2006, p. 78-80).

Lord, give each church and every member a missionary vision!

∼

"While none of us can actually limit or shrink God, we can limit what He does in our lives, and shrink Him in our imaginations"

8

DREAMING BIG

We Serve a Big God

    I look across the beautiful African plains; there is so much to see, and the vision of all that occurs in that expanse is vast. The grasses sway in the wind for miles. The land appears alive, teaming with many species of wildlife which run free. Look, dream, dream big, for we serve a big God. That simple statement of dreaming has a new focus and vision for me since traveling to Kenya, and it is a philosophy my Kenyan friends always seem to have, unlike many American Christians. I learned about dreaming big while in Kenya. My Kenyan friends not only look across those vast plains with a broad vision, but they look upon God with a much greater vision than my eyes ever saw. Too often, in our finite, limited human minds, we shrink God and we try to make Him fit into our little boxes of what we think is possible. We are too often oblivious to the fact that God desires to show us His power, His glory, and His wonder, if we would only open our eyes to see. Look, dream, dream big, for we serve a big God.

    Throughout the Bible, God's people were often placed in difficult, seemingly impossible situations in order for God to show them that it was never their own wisdom, strength or fortitude that carried them through treacherous times, but it was always God at work. The Exodus, which is told multiple times throughout Scripture, shows God performing miracle after miracle for the Israelites in order to allow them to get a glimpse of who He is: a huge, awe-inspiring God whom we will never comprehend, but who wants to take us into the Promised Land. God told Joshua to look out over the Promised Land that he and the Israelites would be entering and to dream big, since God would go before them and allow them to see all He wanted to offer His people. Unfortunately, like an entire generation of the Israelites whom Moses led through the wilderness, many of us never reach the Promised Land for lack of vision, or for lack of faith in living out our vision.

While none of us can actually limit or shrink God, we can limit what He does in our lives, and shrink Him in our imaginations, therefore shrinking and stifling our faith. Peter spoke of the Prophet Joel about the "last days" when believers would be dreaming big:

Then Peter, speaking for the eleven, addressed the crowd with a loud voice, and said, You men of Judaea, and all living in Jerusalem, let me explain this to you, and listen carefully to my words. It is wrong to assume these men are drunk, since it is only nine in the morning. But this is what was prophesied by Joel; when the last days come, I will pour out a portion of My Spirit on mankind: your sons and daughters shall speak forth divine truths, and your young men shall see visions of prophetic significance, and your old men shall experience vivid images of hoped for things even sleeping: 18. and on your believing servants will I pour out of My Spirit, and they shall speak forth under inspiration: (Acts 2:14-18 DNT)

"The last days" refers to the days after the Holy Spirit was given to all people who desired to have Him indwell their being. "Those days," are now. Trust in God who does amazing things. Envision the vast expanse of the African plains, and look, dream, dream big, for we serve a big God.

Here Am I, Send Me

When Jesus instructed us in the *Great Commission* about going into the entire world to make disciples and teach them, I believe He wanted us to be humble, culturally sensitive, loving people who reflect who He is, in whatever culture we serve. R.G. Collingwood wrote, *"For the Christian, all men are equal in the sight of God; there are no chosen people, no privileged race or class, no one community whose fortunes are more important than those of another. All persons and all people are involved in the working out of God's purpose"* (Sanneh, 1989, p. 170).

While the Church in the West is still the strongest economically and politically, the Church in the East and in the Third World, especially Africa, is emerging and growing. We can give to one another whatever God has given to us. The Christian Church is a global Church and we are all united in Jesus Christ, as we respect all human culture as God's gift to humanity. Different people and nations are called to live in, *"Binding covenant relationships of brotherhood. Human beings reach their true end in such relationships, in bonds of mutual love and obedience that reflect the mutual relatedness in love that is the being of the Triune God Himself"* (Bellagamba, 1992, p. 118).

The Church needs to harmonize like a symphony in order to be complete. It must encompass all races, societies, classes and cultures. Jesus Christ is universal and He is viewed differently by different cultures. The various and diverse communities and cultures around the world each produce their own sound, their own voice, and their own music, yet all of them, sounded together, produce the beautiful, complete music of a symphony.

Henri Nouwen wrote a beautiful summary of missions, of which I hope this book reflected:

> *"Here we realize that mission is not only to go and tell others about the risen Lord, but also to receive that witness from those to whom we are sent. Often, mission is thought of exclusively in terms of giving, but true-mission is also receiving. If it is true that the Spirit of Jesus blows where it wants, there is no person who cannot give that Spirit. In the long run, mission is only possible when it is as much receiving as giving, as much being cared for as caring ...But*

we will soon be burned out if we cannot receive the Spirit of the Lord from those to whom we are sent... Each time we reach out, they in turn-whether they are aware or not- will bless us with the Spirit of Jesus and so become our ministers. Without this mutuality of giving and receiving, mission and ministry easily become manipulative or violent. When only one gives and the other receives, the giver will soon become the oppressor and the receivers, victims. But when the giver receives and the receiver gives, the circle of love, begun in the community of the disciples, can grow as wide as the world" (Nouwen, 1994, p.115).

Let the Church and her people "dream big" about missions.

~

AMEN - *so be it*,

An expression of strong agreement and affirmation. The author clearly affirms the content of this book as a needed message to believers.

REFERENCES

Allen, Roland. *Missionary Methods: St. Paul's or Ours?* Michigan: Eerdmans Publishing Co., 1997.

Bellagamba, Anthony. *Mission & Ministry in the Global Church.* New York: Orbis Books, 1992.

Bosch, David J. *Transforming Mission: Paradigm Shifts in Theology of Mission.* New York: Orbis Books, 1991.

Green, Hollis L. *The Evergreen Devotional New Testament (DNT).* Complete Edition, Post-Gutenberg Books: Global Ed Advance Press, 2012.

Haviland, William A. *Cultural Anthropology.* New York: Harcourt Brace College Publishers, 1993.

Hiebert, Paul G. *Cultural Anthropology.* Michigan: Baker Book House, 1976.

Huntington, Samuel P. *The Clash of World Civilizations and the Remaking of the World Order.* New York: Simon & Schuster, 1996.

Janda, Clement. "The Church as Economic Power." *Mission Studies* 13 (1996) 247-254.

Motessi, Dr. Asvoldo. Lecture at Northern Baptist Theological Seminary, Lombard, IL. 2000.

Newbigin, Leslie. *Foolishness to the Greeks.* Michigan: Eerdmans Publishing Co., 1986.

Nieburh, Richard H. *Christ and Culture.* New York: Harper & Row Publishers, 1951.

Nouwen, Henri. *With Burning Hearts: A Meditation on the Eucharistic Life.* New York: Orbis Books, 1994.

Pope Benedict XVI. *Charity in Truth: Caritas in Veritate.* San Francisco: Ignatius Press, 2009.

Pope Benedict XVI. *God is Love.* San Francisco: Ignatius Press, 2006.

Sanneh, Lamin. *Translating the Message: The Missionary Impact on Culture.* New York: Orbis Books, 1989.

The New International Bible (used only for Old Testament quotes).

Weber, Hans-Ruedi. *Salty Christians.* New York: The Seabury Press, 1963.

www.ingramcontent.com/pod-product-compliance
Lightning Source LLC
Chambersburg PA
CBHW031136090426
42738CB00008B/1107